Until now, I had pictured a "mentor" as a kindly old-timer who had nothing better to do than encourage the rookies as they struggled with their fledgling careers. But now, thanks to Hal Johnson's unique book, I have discovered that mentoring is a practical management tool, something that can produce exceptional results across all levels of a company.

Gary W. McDonald, Chairman
Cygnus Marketing Communications, Inc.

This is a refreshing, well-written book that provides the entrepreneurial manager with an invaluable primer full of sound advice that conveys practical insights on motivation and management. The advice is aimed at enhancing the personal careers of employees, while advancing the profit potential of businesses. The sage counsel of successful business entrepreneur Hal Johnson is indispensable for those who lead, implement, or are impacted by corporate strategies. In addition to furnishing thoughtful analyses on how to lead and manage a sustainable enterprise for the long-term competitive advantage, this book provides a clear, pragmatic approach for weaving mentorship into the management of human resources at all levels.

John B. Olsen
Author, Lecturer and Business Advisor

Mentoring for Exceptional Performance *delivers a dose of reality from an executive who has successfully led and grown business organizations, where development of human talent is critical. Hal provides a "back to basics" approach to mentoring that involves accountability, warmth and genuine concern for developing leaders. An excellent addition to the management library.*

Roger L. Pringle, President
The Pringle Company

We all have mentors from time to time. Sometimes we realize it, sometimes we don't. Hal makes a strong case for formalizing the process. Planned, targeted mentoring, such as Hal describes, ensures ongoing business success. Hal served as my management mentor for years without ever using the word "mentor." As I read his book, I experienced renewed appreciation for what he did for me. Many of the management and character principles that Hal demonstrated are now among my habits.

Ron Martin, Author and President
Success Dynamics, Inc.

A home run!! A powerful and proven process to enrich the human performance of any organization.

Tom Ocasek, Former President
Delco Remy, Inc.

Do you want to make a lasting difference in the history of your organization? In the lives of those on your team? Mentoring for Exceptional Performance is an unusual business book—based on an elegantly simple concept. It challenges you to change the way you see yourself in relationship to your organization and your peers. The mentoring principle is not new, but for the first time, clear steps are outlined to make the most of this powerful process. The message is clear: If you want to build your organization to last, you must build up the people on your team.

Lani Williams
Director of Communications
NW Medical Teams International

Hal's book has captured in print a step-by-step process that leaders of any organization can use to develop relationships that will empower everyone to accomplish the missions for which they exist. His processes are timeless, proven and effective. If you want to develop the full potential of your staff, this is a "must-read" book.

Donald A. Jensen, Senior Pastor
Village Baptist Church

Hal Johnson has written an outstanding book on mentoring and its importance in building and strengthening management teams. It is a superior treatment of the subject, with directly applicable guidelines for developing mentoring programs,— whether formal or informal—within organizations. Having been mentored by Hal during my first six years in the corporate world, I have experienced first-hand how beneficial a properly managed mentoring relationship can be.

Brick Thompson, CEO
Business Management Company, Inc.

I believe Hal has connected with the heart and addresses many of the reasons why businesses fail. He has created a logical, organized methodology to solve a critical business issue.

Kurt S. Glassman, Principal
Pacific Advisory Group

Hal has been there and done what he advocates—mentored teams toward exceptional performance. His book provides insight for those who are motivated to seriously improve the individual member as well as the whole team. His is a book that will not just be read, but will become a mentoring reference. It is a winner—without a doubt.

Charles E. Carlbom, Chairman
BPI—Business Projects Inc.

MENTORING

FOR

EXCEPTIONAL

PERFORMANCE

Harold E. Johnson

Griffin Publishing
Glendale, California

Editorial Statement

In the interest of brevity and unencumbered prose, the editor has chosen to use the standard English form of address. This usage is not meant to suggest that the content of this book, both in its references and to whom it is addressed, is intended as restrictive or exclusive regarding any individual or group of individuals, whether by gender, race, age, or any other means that might be considered discriminatory.

Publisher: Robert Howland
Director of Operations: Robin Howland
Managing Editor: Marjorie L. Marks
Book Design: Mark M. Dodge
Cover Design: Patty Bruner

10 9 8 7 6 5 4 3 2 1

ISBN 1-882180-83-6

Griffin Publishing
544 Colorado Street
Glendale, California 91204

Telephone: (818) 244-1470

Manufactured in the United States of America

Acknowledgments

Writing a book has helped me realize a number of important lessons. Perhaps the most significant is the power of collaboration. Like many aspiring writers, when I started this project, I thought I could knock out a fairly decent draft in a few months. That was two years ago. I was running a company at the same time, so I had to grab whatever time I could to write. Because I could only write in short spurts, in the beginning my writing was, shall we say, somewhat uneven. In addition, the book wasn't fully conceptualized.

Fortunately, my son, Brad, reviewed my efforts in the early stages. Brad holds degrees in engineering and law and he is very disciplined. His written communication is startlingly clean, crisp and clear. He provided invaluable guidance regarding the structure of the book. Thanks again, Brad. Receiving your guidance was a wonderful experience.

June Hill, my U.K. secretary, was inspirational, as she always is. Her adept handling of humor/humour never allowed me to take myself too seriously. A big thanks for being who you are.

My good friend and colleague at Private Capital, Dick Buxton, played a key role in the book's development. He saw an early draft of some of the material I use for training and encouraged me to write the book. If only I had known...

As the author of *You've Built A Successful Business—Now What?* Dick was kind enough to introduce me to his publisher. A special thanks to you, Dick, for your encouragement and support—in all things.

It was a distinct privilege to work with my editor, Marjorie Marks. What a joy it was to have had her guidance and input. Her contribution to clarity has been immense. She is a most gracious, sensitive and intelligent mentor. I wish I could have taken her "course" at the start of this process. Any deficiencies, however, still are mine.

Two other folks at Griffin Publishing were immensely helpful and supportive. A very special thanks to Robin Howland and Bob Howland.

Two very special colleagues at LionHeart Consulting in Portland, Oregon were most helpful in reviewing the material in Chapter Eleven relating to behavior assessment. A warm thank you to Karen Howells and Paul Werder for their insights.

My colleagues (past and present), reviewers, commentators and teammates in my life adventures have made significant contributions toward bringing this material to book form. A special thanks to Brad Lyons and Ron Martin for their in-depth reviews, comments and suggestions. And a big mahalo to Charles Lau for cover design assistance.

For their contributions to this project, I also express deep appreciation to Kurt Glassman, Jim Grant, Brick Thompson, Ed Sultan, Jr., Nick Nagel, Dave Jeffery, Tom Ocasek, Rick Ralston, Bob Midkiff, Jeff Walters, Roger Pringle, Gary McDonald, Jay Fountain, Gerry Czarnechi, Dan Wilson, Vernon Woo, Ed Sultan, III, Jere Smith, Bud Lindstrand, Bob Walker, Don Jensen, Craig and Marjorie Walsh, Nigel MacLennon, Cindy Hudson, Lani Williams, John Olsen, Chuck Carlbom, Neil Goldschmidt, Kevin Sorensen, Tim Guard, Glyn Davies, and last, but certainly not least, my very favorite critic, Adeline Johnson.

And for those who have mentored me through special portions of life's adventure, my sincere gratitude to you: John Olsen, John Coombs, Don Jensen, Roger Lageschulte and Bill Ritchie.

To you all, I am deeply indebted. Thanks so much for your friendship, support and encouragement. For you all, I wish exceptional results.

To Adeline

My best friend, wife and
valued colleague.
Thank you for helping create
four decades of bliss.

*"All my fellow townsmen know you
are a woman of noble character"*

—Ruth 3:11

Preface

All businesses are in transition. Some are in positive transition, yet many (perhaps most!) are not. Businesses that were originally started by entrepreneurs often begin to fizzle when they outgrow the management abilities of their founders.

What does it take, then, for a business to successfully make the transition to a bigger arena? How do you retain the entrepreneurial spirit while still tapping into shared management and leadership principles? How do you meet the challenges of super-heated change in the marketplace? Can it be done without throwing out the entrepreneur? The answer is yes, if he or she is willing to change the business culture—and make some personal changes, too. Change of this magnitude often requires strategic mentoring.

Managing change through strategically mentoring growth is the focus of this book. To prepare an organization for the future, there are three key areas of mentoring focus that need to impact the entire organization: learning, leading and relating. Revolutionary? Perhaps to the entrepreneur. Yet, while the principles are centuries old, they also are very effective if one wishes to create a culture that not only supports exceptional performance, but thrives on it.

For the last twenty-five years I have been "transitioning" businesses. In several instances, we helped develop new business cultures after the businesses had outgrown their entrepreneurs. In the process, we have discovered that certain principles are necessary to enable an organization to be "transitioned" into a super performer. It's not easy, but it can be done.

As the chief executive officer of five different companies during the course of my business career, including most recently a United Kingdom company, my specialty is to bring companies and organizations to high-performance mode through a specific process of transition. I am a transition manager, an experienced professional in building performance cultures.

Mentoring for Exceptional Performance describes how managers at all levels can transform their businesses by using the principles described in this book. If properly implemented, these principles enable companies to achieve exceptional, perhaps extraordinary, performances. So, primarily this book is for managers. But wait. That doesn't mean only manager-type managers. Nearly everyone is a manager, responsible for managing something or someone. It doesn't matter whether you manage the household, the carpool, a den of cub scouts, a square dance club, a reading group or a large corporation. The material presented in the following pages will challenge your thinking about how you can perform your management responsibilities with even greater effectiveness. Although *Mentoring for Exceptional Performance* is oriented toward the private business sector, these concepts are useful in a broad range of management situations, including governments, schools, hospitals, nonprofit organizations, and, as indicated above, even the family.

While I have used the male gender throughout this book as a matter of convention and ease, the material is aimed at both sexes and is as relevant for the housewife running the home as much as it is for the husband running the business or the househusband running the home and the wife running the business. Rules and roles are changing, along with many other aspects of our lives. Regardless of your personal involvement with management, I hope the principles presented in these pages will stimulate your own thoughts about what can be done to achieve not only better results, but exceptional results. This game is open to all who may be interested in a systematic process of enriching the performance capability of those who deliver results—people like you and me. This really is a case of "one size fits all."

THE THREE-FOLD OBJECTIVES OF THIS BOOK

1. To present information explaining the potential benefits of mentoring—at all levels and in a broad range of settings—and how mentoring prepares the organization and its individual members to meet the future (the *why*).

2. To provide insights and direction for establishing a comprehensive mentoring program and what it "looks like" (the *what*).

3. To present information that enables the reader to understand the critical elements of an effective mentoring program and the essential steps necessary to create a mentoring organization (the *how*).

A comprehensive mentoring strategy can be the driving force in developing an organization's work force potential. Somehow, the possible economic benefits of developing people have escaped the notice of many managers, shareholders and business owners. Yet there is a strong connection between people development and financial performance. Far too many businesses are achieving only 70 percent to 80 percent of what they should be achieving just because their human resources are not running in an efficient and effective mode. This situation is comparable to running an engine with one of the spark plug wires disconnected. The major costs are already being borne in the people costs. Helping people achieve what they already should be achieving is merely astute investing. Connect those loose spark plug wires! The costs of not doing so are just too great.

Hal Johnson
Portland, Oregon

Foreword

Hal Johnson is a former client, a close friend and now a valued partner. During a period in which he was a client and CEO of a very large private company, I was impressed by his ability to bring people together and provide one-on-one mentoring for key management people to ensure solid growth.

Hal has the skills and the experience of an educator and leader—with a firm but gentle hand. When he left our client firm to assume senior executive responsibility with a company in the UK, we continued our friendship and I spent time with him in England, where he brought together a lot of people who needed direction. He also has assumed responsibility for helping clients develop a mentoring process within their companies to bring along talented people to eventually assume the leadership responsibilities necessary for viable management succession.

With his background in government and in private business (both domestic and international), and his continuing quest to understand how people emerge from followership to assume leadership responsibility, he is unique. His intellectual curiosity and his ability to help people define their individual and collective visions and missions make him a truly effective senior advisor for those organizations with the wisdom to integrate management development into business perpetuation planning.

The most powerful force in human affairs is the realizable wish. Hal has an uncommon ability to help people create their personal "wish list," develop their goals, and then map out a strategy for their achievement.

Dickson C. Buxton
Managing Director
Private Capital Corporation

CONTENTS

PART I

THE CASE FOR MENTORING

CHAPTERS 1-5

CHAPTER ONE

INTRODUCTION TO MENTORING

OVERVIEW

A recent Wall Street Journal article about mentoring in the workplace reported that nine out of ten workers who had ever received any kind of job coaching or mentoring found it helpful. Astonishingly, however, among those polled, only 38 percent had ever received any kind of mentoring!

Life is like that. So many things would be good for us—if only we did them or had access to them. Have you ever noticed the difference between people who know the right things to do—and do them—and others who also know the right things to do, but don't do them? The "doers" of physical fitness, for example, usually are more energetic and vibrant, and seem to exude something most other people lack. The difference is that when they decide to do something "extra" to get what they want, they actually do it.

Comparable situations exist in business, where the literature contains much good information on how we can make our businesses more successful—if only we follow through. Unfortunately, most businesses, like most individuals, do not leave their comfort zone until they are confronted with crisis. Many people put forth that extra effort required to attain physical fitness only after receiving some form of health warning, otherwise known as the old "wake-up call."

Attaining and retaining business fitness is the subject of this book. Anyone who runs a business, whether as an entrepreneur or a manager, knows the job is not getting any easier—and succeeding in business has never been easy. Because society is changing so rapidly, you can never take your eye off the ball. Today's fast-ball game of business requires sharper instincts, innovative strategizing and creative teamwork.

The key competitive weapon of the future, according to Lester Thurow, Dean of MIT's Sloan School of Management and author of *Head To Head,* will be the skills of the work force. Brain power creates new technologies, but it will be skilled workers who allow companies to actually use these cutting-edge products and processes. A skilled work force is becoming a company's most important means of leverage in the competitive marketplace.

——— ◇ ———

The key competitive weapon of the future will be the work force.

——— ◇ ———

Mentoring for Exceptional Performance is a guide for preparing your human resources to compete at the highest levels, which requires a well-conceived strategy and excellent execution. This book will lead you through the thought processes and action steps necessary to create a powerful business force based on management-driven mentoring. When implemented properly, this strategy will prepare your business to compete at an olympic level. And it shouldn't take a business crisis to get you started.

MESSAGE TO MANAGERS

Very often, terms that are used in business, such as mentoring, become part of the general lexicon without their specific or originally intended meanings accompanying their popularization. For this reason, I wish to clarify my definition of mentoring as it relates to the business environment:

MENTORING DEFINED

Mentoring means to facilitate, guide and encourage continuous innovation, learning and growth to prepare the business for the future. Mentoring in business is most effective when discretely targeted at three levels: 1) the individual workers; 2) the management team and the other working groups; 3) the entire organization and its culture.

While many people use the terms "mentoring" and "coaching" interchangeably, I make a distinction between them: Essentially, coaching is a subset of mentoring. Mentoring focuses on growth and development on a global or macro level, while coaching usually refers to specific skill development, such as public speaking or the art of delegation. There is much overlap, and both are essential and inseparable. The focus of this book, however, is mentoring—creating a strategy for comprehensive growth and development.

Let's look at mentoring in the broader context. More than forty years ago, Peter Drucker published his milestone classic, *The Practice of Management,* which remains a fundamental work in identifying the essential tasks of a manager. Drucker's five basic management functions (setting objectives, organizing, motivating and communicating, measuring, and developing people) are as valid today as they were in 1955. Yet the one primary task that seems to be continually neglected by managers is the development of people.

Human-resource development consists of a series of planned processes that identify, utilize and develop people in ways that strengthen individual and organizational effectiveness. They incorporate training, coaching, mentoring and related activities aimed at individual growth and development. For optimal results, it is extremely important that the process be supported and led by senior management.

Basically, all development is self-development. Consequently, if the individual is not motivated at a personal level, then development usually does not occur. The manager is responsible for facilitating this development process. It is in this vein that I recommend mentoring the entire organization for which a manager has responsibility, as a way to create a powerful development force. Leading a group of individuals who are excited about developing their abilities and their careers provides astonishing rewards—both for the individuals and the company.

THE NEW ERA—CHANGE

One of the more significant effects of accelerating change in business and in society is the unprecedented amount of information that has become widely available. We are in the midst of an information explosion that is forever changing the world and the way it does business. Never before has it been so difficult to keep up with the business environment.

A strategy is essential. Unless there is some effective process to lead and direct ongoing innovation and learning, businesses risk being left behind. Managers must have a strategy that enables them to stay abreast of the rapid flow of business knowledge, while simultaneously maintaining a vision that energetically carries the organization forward. This requires the resources of a motivated, knowledgable work force focused on growth and development—corporately *and* personally.

———— ◇ ————

Mentoring is one of the most effective means of accomplishing perpetual innovation and learning.

———— ◇ ————

Mentoring is not a quick fix, a fad or an experiment. Yet comprehensive, organization-wide mentoring is one of the most effective means of accomplishing perpetual innovation and learning.

The concept is centuries-old. We first see an account of it in the book of Proverbs in the Old Testament, which, according to scholars, dates from the 10th century B.C. The peace and prosperity that characterized that era accord well with the development of reflective wisdom and the production of literary works. A careful look at Proverbs reveals that most of our management imperatives can be found in some form in this profound literature. Although the term "mentor" is first seen in Homer's *Odyssey*, in Proverbs the term "counselor" is descriptive of the same process.

MENTORING—MY DISCOVERY

THE MOMENT OF NEED

In the early seventies, I held the position of Director of Management Services for the City of Portland, Oregon. I was working for a very energetic, young, intelligent mayor who set a direction that really stretched my abilities. As the chief administrative specialist in the city organization, I was expected to have most of the management answers.

A problem arose that convinced me I needed the assistance of an experienced management advisor. After a concerted effort, I was fortunate to meet John Olsen, who had been with one of the major New York-based management consulting firms. At the time, John was involved in management-development consulting for the governor of the state of Ohio. He agreed to help me resolve my problem. Although we began working together on that particular problem, eventually the work relationship developed into a mentoring process.

EXPANDED PERSPECTIVE

At our first meeting, I described the specific challenge I was facing at that moment. John immediately went to the white board and started writing. I was astonished. Here was a guy who knew little or nothing about my particular problem, yet through a series of questions, answers, "what ifs" and the like, he was able to put his finger on the root issues and suggest possible strategies. Based on the success of our first meeting, I arranged to meet with John on a monthly basis. I would begin these meetings by describing several issues or problems and John would proceed with a series of questions and hypothetical situations that often made me wonder, "Why didn't I think of that?"

During those months of our working together, John consistently supplied me with reading material that gave me additional perspectives on the challenges with which I was grappling. Our relationship was instrumental in opening numerous intellectual windows for me. It commenced my lifelong quest to learn as much as possible about this "stuff" we generally call management.

My discovery of the mentoring process was, indeed, serendipitous. John and I began by looking for a solution to a particular problem and ended with my discovery of mentoring. Fortunately for me, I was able to continue my "mentee" relationship with John as my career took me from one place to another. Over many years, John served as my sounding board and main resource for dealing with the problems I encountered. We even solved many problems over the telephone when face-to-face meetings were not possible. The ability to tap into a growth resource on an as-needed basis has had profound and lasting benefit for me, facilitating a rich, fast-paced career-development process.

Occasionally we even discussed issues touching my personal life and, always, I found John's thinking and contributions both engaging and challenging. He made me think. He also put me on the path toward discovering how effective I could be in helping other managers develop their skills and careers through mentoring.

BETTER RESULTS

Twenty-five years later, I consider it a privilege to have served as a mentor to many former and current colleagues. Becoming a mentor has been gratifying and rewarding in many ways, though perhaps the greatest benefit is that I found mentoring to be one of the best methods for developing managers and leaders. I actively encourage young managers who also are interested in a rich and fast-paced career development process to find not just *a* mentor, but the *right* mentor; one capable of providing both guidelines for growth and dynamic feedback and encouragement.

CHANGING BUSINESS ENVIRONMENT

Preparing for the inevitable—change—is smart management because planning leads to choices rather than the constraints inherent in management-by-crisis. Unfortunately, businesses frequently are more like people who fall into the river of life and get swept along, helpless to control where they finally land. The amount of white water in the river of business life is on the upsurge. Navigating the changing conditions has become increasingly treacherous, requiring extreme skill and superb conditioning. I have found that the best way to meet the challenges presented by a rapidly changing business environment is through mentoring.

LEADING THE CULTURE

People in business have had to make enormous changes in the past decade. The truth is that we are all really in the knowledge business now, a point made by Bill Gates in his book, *The Road Ahead*. Business is shifting its work-process emphasis from "task processing" to processes based on the use of finite knowledge. Managing knowledge workers is much different from managing task workers. In fact, you don't really manage knowledge workers—they manage themselves. Enlightened executives understand that, and, as a result, make a distinction between *managing* and *leading*. They know that *leading* increasingly is displacing *managing* in the knowledge environment.

I had an opportunity to observe a facet of this process when a very large American company acquired a mid-market-sized business in the United Kingdom. The U.K. company was entrepreneurially spawned and still had much of the "zip" created by its founders. Major portions of the business were comprised of knowledge workers. Really talented knowledge workers (and who wants any other kind?) are more effectively led than managed. Period.

Well, on Day One under the new ownership, the high-ranking executive team from the new company held several informational meetings to make introductions and describe the new culture. It was an excellent idea. But the top executive got off on the wrong foot, particularly from the point-of-view of the knowledge workers. When he described the new culture, it seemed to be strongly slanted toward, "This is the way it will, or will not, be done...or else." Hmmm.

—— ◇ ——

Leading increasingly is displacing *managing* in the knowledge environment.

—— ◇ ——

The person on the platform undoubtedly wanted to do the right thing. He is a very successful executive with a great track record. And I was sure the matter would be resolved over time. Yet, I make this point to highlight the need for awareness when "managing" knowledge workers. Issuing ultimatums is ineffective and can be disastrous. We want to facilitate the kind of development and leadership culture that challenges our bright colleagues to do the right things (and the bright things) because they just know those are the things to do.

Related to the subject of constraints and creativity is a fascinating scenario found in the breakdown of communism and the emergence of free-market economies. As a player and collector of mandolin family instruments, I had occasion to visit Prague in the Czech Republic, where a very talented luthier was crafting a mandolin to my order. My wife and I spent several days with instrument maker George Lebeda and his family, and, during our stay, engaged in numerous conversations about the historical transition occurring in their society. We discussed the differences before and after the 1991 Velvet Revolution (precipitated by what has come to be reverently and affectionately known as Prague Spring), the peaceful transition from communism to democracy. As a student of human behavior, I wanted to know more about the dreams, thoughts, and reactions of the people prior to and following the Revolution. It seemed clear to us that their visions and actions on behalf of freedom had released collective creative energy, leading to the revolution to end oppression. All of this has relevance for the kind of enlightened leadership style, laced with encouragement and freedom, that stimulates creativity in a knowledge environment.

PREPARING FOR THE FUTURE

Essentially, I advocate mentoring to create change and foster renewal, which means to guide and strengthen the culture of a business through the processes of leading, learning and relating. It is through these three processes that an organization can be energized to create a successful future.

Those who have been in management for very long know that simply encouraging these kinds of processes does not guarantee that they will happen. Someone has to drive them. By driving them, I am not suggesting coercion. However, there needs to be a disciplined process, managed sensitively, to enable the organization to absorb new awarenesses and knowledge in order to prepare for change and renewal. And I firmly believe that mentoring is the enabling process.

Mentoring does not mean pressuring anyone to do anything. Capable and intelligent colleagues usually respond quickly to good ideas properly presented. Yet, merely circulating memos pointing out how important change and renewal are to future success is unlikely to give you the desired results. Otherwise, all we would need to do is circulate all the available good business information that supports what we want done. Rather, as manager-leaders we need to be sensitive in facilitating the process.

———— ◇ ————

Success does not happen by chance.
Success requires a well-executed strategy.
Mentoring facilitates that strategy.

———— ◇ ————

Book Structure and Overview

The balance of the material in this book is aimed at helping you understand the power of mentoring and the ways it can be used.

Part I, A Case For Mentoring, contains five chapters, including this one, in which the case is made for mentoring in business. Change is addressed as a increasingly important issue for business. Strategic change is examined. The Strategic Mentoring Model and how it works is discussed. Finally, material is presented on how to launch and manage a comprehensive mentoring program.

Part II, Whom to Mentor, explains, in three separate chapters, whom to mentor and the processes involved in the mentoring of individuals, groups and organizations.

Then *Part III, What to Mentor,* includes three chapters that present the case for the critical mentoring content: learning, leading and relating.

Part IV, The Way Forward, brings the book to a close with a review of the essential steps involved in becoming a mentor, a separate chapter on becoming a mentee, and the final chapter on creating a preferred future through mentoring.

That is only a brief overview of the structure involved in mentoring. The material itself includes anecdotes and stories that illustrate my philosophy. When you read that I have had more than thirty years' management experience, you may wonder whether that means one year, thirty times; or perhaps five years, six times. Managing as many diverse situations as I have has not allowed me to relive many of the same years. My career has been an adventure in which I have purposely targeted the three- to five-year engagements. There have been longer ones when ownership was involved. I have sought the opportunities (or they have sought me) that usually required learning a lot about the new business as quickly as possible. Undoubtedly, that catapulted me down the path of continuous learning. But most important, I discovered the power of mentoring. It has been an exciting adventure. And I have learned a lot about what creates successful business results. I hope in these pages to communicate to you important lessons to enhance your own adventure toward success in your chosen career.

To aid the learning process, I have included a few questions at the end of each chapter. (No, this is not a quiz.) They are aimed at triggering responses that come from deep thinking. The kind of thinking that engenders bright futures.

MENTOR'S CHECKUP

◇ How much of your management focus is directed toward building your human resource?

◇ How are your colleagues preparing to meet the business demands over the next two or three years? How about you?

◇ How much management-learning material (other than news) do you read each year? Each month? Each week?

◇ Having just read Chapter One, what are the implications of *not* having a viable, systematic learning-and-development program in your organization?

◇ What could you or your organization do differently?

CHAPTER TWO

CHANGE HAPPENS!

OVERVIEW

Business literature is doing a fine job of calling attention to the significant amount of change that is occurring. Most business people realize that change has accelerated significantly in the past decade and is a force to be reckoned with. Like many things in life, change is what we make of it. We know change will happen, so we can either be proactive and prepare for it or, instead, react to it after the fact. Intellectually, everyone would agree with the necessity to plan. In fact, *not* planning is equivalent to deciding not to act, allowing external events or individuals to decide the fate of your business by default. Yet it is amazing how often this is allowed to happen. In business, this will occur at a diminishing rate because passive managers won't be around to repeat the mistake. Business leaders who survive will be those who respond proactively and strategically. Not only will they be prepared for change, they will make it an ally. A good "change" strategy can do that. And mentoring is a key element in an effective "change" strategy.

Unfortunately, when business leaders confront the challenges presented by a changing business environment, they often are uncertain about what to do next, particularly when preparation has been inadequate.

In this chapter, both successful and unsuccessful business-change response patterns will be described. We will then focus on how successful business leaders prepare for change and, indeed, *embrace* change as a catalyst for success.

—— ◇ ——

**When change is viewed as catalyst
rather than threat, the entire management culture can
be mentored to prepare for and seize the opportunities
that accompany change.**

—— ◇ ——

CORE ISSUE—CHANGE OR GET LEFT BEHIND

Every time I read a newspaper, another business book, spend time with my children and grandchildren, or look in the mirror, I am reminded of the unalterable fact that everything changes. Most change occurs so gradually (like my receding hairline) that we hardly notice the process. And yet to ignore, wittingly or not, the fact that change is occurring, is to possibly doom your career, your organization, perhaps even your life.

The older we become, the more important it is to have regular health examinations. As we know, life-threatening problems, if they exist, often can be eliminated or controlled at this point. Without precautionary awareness, however, the fate of your health is entirely—rather than only partially—based on luck. Personal-health decision-making represents an apt metaphor for business-health decision-making. In each situation, passivity can, at worst, prove fatal; at best, not only can you head off disaster, you can optimistically plan for the future.

Not only is business experiencing revolutionary change, but these changes are complex. (Since so much already has been written on this subject, I refer you to the bibliography at the end of the book for further reading material.) The business environment faces more threats—and opportunities—than ever before. How best can businesses cope?

———— ◇ ————

Anticipation creates the best kind of preparedness.
And anticipation is a continuous process.

———— ◇ ————

The answer is to consider prevention strategy, using the paradigm of the healthcare industry, which has focused on ways to prosper from change. Health insurance companies seem to have been the catalysts rather than the victims of change. In fact, to the average person it seems that all the rules of the new healthcare game are theirs. While business, in general, is underinformed about the forces of change, the healthcare industry is both sophisticated and proactive in directing, leading, and even creating change. In other words, rather than coping with superimposed change, as it seems most other businesses/industries must, the healthcare industry itself may be viewed as a change-catalyst, unlike the average hapless business about to be sideswiped by change that it hasn't seen coming.

Such a strategy has its foundation in anticipation. The implicit question becomes, "What else should we do?"

CREATING AND MAINTAINING A SUCCESSFUL BUSINESS

Unless we have a deliberate strategy to deal with change, change will deal with us. Preparedness not only requires a strategy for change, but a changing strategy. While change is inevitable, its impact cannot be fully assessed before the fact. Therefore, the best approach is to create a strategy to cope with and prosper from change. Rather than a static strategy, such as one that is based on a given percentage increase in market share, for example, the strategy should focus on the "delivery system"—the people. The most potent strategy will focus on building the resource that will acquire not only market share, but more important, create the business products and processes that drive the business success.

My management roles have varied, but generally I have been recruited to meet what I call a business perpetuation need that is the consequence of a serious financial condition, a consolidation, a merger, or the necessity for a company to "transition" into a larger corporate entity. These experiences have introduced me to numerous environments, each with different needs. Yet, the threads of many common issues are woven through disparate business situations.

The variety of situations and challenges my career has offered has been exciting. My positions have allowed me to manage businesses operating in the U.S., Japan, Great Britain, Ireland, France, Australia and New Zealand. In these management roles, I have encountered just about every type of personality, behavioral issue, systems fault, cultural problem, or business crisis you can imagine. And yes, I have enjoyed the adventure (if not the problems themselves). My delight and fulfillment comes from seeing managers become excited about their work and in producing exceptional results in spite of problems. And that essentially has been my focus. To build and mentor management teams that can create successes beyond the abilities of the component team members.

Change patterns fall into two categories: patterns for failure or patterns for success. In the various positions I have held, my responsibilities and opportunities were created by the need to turn near-failures or serious problems into successes. At the heart of each pattern—whether of failure or of success—is change.

MAJOR PATTERNS OF FAILURE

THE BUSINESS OUTGROWS MANAGEMENT

This is among the most common of business crises. Simply stated, the problems just get too big for the capabilities of the resident management. Further, many of the "too big problems" were spawned by the resident management, albeit inadvertently. Too often decisions were poorly supported by research and evaluation. Usually, there was an entrepreneur involved who still wanted to make most, if not all, of the decisions. Such situations are compounded when a business is experiencing rapid growth. There are numerous variations on the theme, but the key problem is underskilled management attempting to handle the complexities of a growing business in an ever-changing business environment.

My first encounter with this last type of business problem occurred during my first CEO appointment. The business was in deep financial trouble, which included a multimillion-dollar loss the prior year, the union was in near revolt, morale was too low to measure, the existing department heads were, for all intents and purposes, in different businesses, since they were not speaking to one another. There were differing opinions on the board of directors regarding some of the solutions to the problems. Yes, I was recruited, not gang-pressed into the CEO spot. I researched how "do-able" the job was before accepting the position. This included interviewing all the department heads, the company's lawyers and accountants, as well as several of the board members. The turnaround wasn't easy. But *we* did it. It took more than two years to get back into the black. It required a major revamping of the management team. Out of five department heads, two were replaced and one new manager was hired to head a department created with functions reallocated from one of the existing departments. An entire new culture had to be created. And the essential, and somewhat fundamental, skills that had been absent had to be found. Had they been present prior to my arrival, I probably would not have had this fantastic opportunity.

The organization had fallen into the trap of the book-keeper becoming the accountant, then the senior accountant, then the chief accountant, then the controller—and yes, finally even the vice-president of finance—all without any training or acquisition of new knowledge or skills. To truly appreciate the magnitude of the problem, multiply this situation times ten or twelve. I had previously only read about this kind of situation. Unfortunately, such circumstances diminish both the businesses and the employees.

On another occasion, I was invited to become the chief executive of a company in the Pacific Northwest that owned thirteen cable television franchises. It was operated by an entrepreneur who had started with virtually nothing and had created a very valuable business over about a twenty-year period. In the last three or four years, through acquisition of additional franchises, the business had grown rapidly. When I arrived, management was in disarray because the entrepreneur was spending more time looking at international opportunities than in running the business. Which was why he hired me—to provide basic general management of this fundamentally sound business. What I discovered was that the business was experiencing an extremely tight cash flow because of the rapid growth. Further complicating matters was the fact that the rapid growth was being handled in an unsophisticated manner. The business had been divided into three basic departments—Finance, Operations, and Sales & Service. Unfortunately, the system that was being constructed to distribute the cable television signals was not in accordance with programming that customers were ordering. The electronic components being ordered by the operations engineers generated the wrong frequencies to deliver the programming being ordered by the pro-gramming staff. The level of knowledge and expertise required to coordinate the more complex activities of this growing, technically oriented business exceeded the skills of those with responsibility for executing the tasks. The business demands had exceeded the managers' knowledge and skills. Fortunately, the business environment had been very forgiving. Cash flow was predictable, albeit somewhat thin in relation to some of the construction requirements. It took about a year-and-a-half to create a smooth-running operation with a competent management team at the helm.

To solve the problems, a very systematic approach was taken. The key functions were identified. Key manage-ment changes were made to assure that skilled managers were focusing on critical functions. The beginnings of a management team emerged. Next the critical systems that supported the key functions were documented and evaluated. Then we asked, "What else can we do to make it better?" It became fun to show up and take on the next challenge. The business results became more predictable. And more positive. Eventually, we were rewarded with an attractive offer for the business from one of the major players in the industry. There were two happy endings: a successful turnaround and the subsequent sale to one of the major national cable television companies.

In both of these turnaround situations, there was absolutely no prior human-resource development in place. Very fundamental business practices were not in place. No investment in the people had been made. There was no change strategy. As soon as these deficiencies were addressed, the business results immediately improved. No big surprise.

THE ENTREPRENEUR FAILS TO TRANSITION MANAGEMENT

The fact is that we cannot do without entrepreneurs. They take us where conservative, practiced business managers would never go. And they do it with huge amounts of success. I have watched three such entrepreneurs create businesses. I remain in awe of their tenacity and special genius. They accomplished business feats I only dream about. Unfortunately, they did not stop quite soon enough. Ah yes, timing. Their successes soon created business demands that exceeded their management skills.

Most entrepreneurs consider the need to deal with business analyses, team building, meetings and the discipline necessary to guide a growing business as bureaucratic nonsense. At this point, most entrepreneurs decide it's no longer fun and they go on to something else. A slight variation on this theme occurs when the entrepreneur just does not have enough hours in the day to allow the same management practices to continue, so it is no longer feasible or fun to maintain the pace. He or she is just overwhelmed with too many decisions for one person. If their timing is right, they still have a viable business to sell. If not, they suffer a serious business setback, or even loss of the business.

Most entrepreneurs enjoy making the decisions and, as a result, feel compelled to make all or most of the significant ones. Therefore, seldom do they see the need for the development of decision-making capacity among the management personnel. I have inherited some "stunted" managers who were quite frustrated about the situation and anxious to develop their decision-making and management skills as quickly as possible. This called for "fast-track" management development. In one situation, I convened the senior management staff (about thirty individuals) for two to three hours a week for six months to assure that the business fundamentals were commonly understood. It was really fun. And the participants were excited about the opportunities for growth.

It was essentially in this context that I discovered team mentoring. What started out as a group exercise spawned rudiments of team focus and performance. Watching a management team "gel" is still one of my more enjoyable life experiences.

THE CHANGING MARKETPLACE

A third scenario involves the core business itself. A great product or service is the basis for the existence of the business and contributes to significant success in the early days. Then the market changes, the business responds too slowly, and momentum is lost—or worse. A recent business adventure involved a financial services company in Great Britain. The founding entrepreneurs found a niche service opportunity that existed in the U.S. but had not yet found its way to the U.K. These two brilliant and hard-working entrepreneurs forged a tremendous financial-service business success over a seven-year period. Then an alternative financial service was introduced by the banking community. Initially, the impact was not significant, but it became increasingly so after a couple of years. Still, the impact was not devastating. The business just ceased to grow, and in fact, began a slight decline. New product research and development was understaffed and underemphasized. Notably, this was the domain of the entrepreneurs, so little experience and responsibility existed elsewhere in the company. Momentum was lost in offsetting the results of the diminishing product with a new product. No disaster; just lost momentum and profits. In this case, management was slow to respond to a changing market. Essentially, the entrepreneurs had ignored the importance of resource development by failing to train and develop the marketing staff to respond to its changing environment. As in many entrepreneurial environments, the staff was young and inexperienced. They were unprepared to deal with the problem. And the entrepreneurs had begun to distance themselves from the day-to-day operations. The problem was addressed and the business moved on, fortunately. In many businesses the ending is less positive.

—— ◇ ——

The key issue here is not only the need
to respond quickly to fluctuating market conditions,
but the need to proactively be prepared to adjust
at the earliest signs of change.

—— ◇ ——

Businesses need to keep one eye on the horizon and one on the ball. This is where a well-trained, proactive and responsive staff can contribute much. Which brings us to the successful side of change.

MAJOR PATTERNS OF SUCCESS

VISIONARY COMPANIES

A few years ago two Stanford University professors, James Collins and Jerry Porras, wrote a fascinating book titled, *Built to Last*. It presented the results of a six-year research project conducted by the Stanford Graduate School of Business, which studied visionary companies- not charismatic, visionary leaders, or visionary product concepts or incredible marketing insights. The central theme is something far more important, substantial and enduring: visionary *companies.* The authors took an in-depth look at eighteen exceptional and long-lasting companies. They compared each company to one of its top competitors. Their objective was to find out what makes the truly exceptional companies different from other companies. Near the completion of their project, the two authors wanted to dispel the false, but widely accepted idea, that only charismatic visionary managers, entrepreneurs and leaders can build visionary companies. And they found data to support their viewpoint and conclusions.

—— ◇ ——

The *business culture* of truly exceptional and enduring companies is systematically established through its human resources.

—— ◇ ——

What Collins and Porras concluded is that major successes are created as a result of being an *organizational* visionary and building the *characteristics* of a visionary company. The authors point to the methodology that the framers of our Constitution used to develop a system or a process that would give us good presidents long after its visionary authors were gone. The process is based on principles related to human ideals and values and is sensitive to human needs and aspirations. In other words, it is a system with a *spirit.* The writers conclude that the *business culture* of truly exceptional and enduring companies is systematically established through its human resources, which perpetuate the business. Such spirit-oriented companies thrive for an average of nearly 100 years, and, since 1926, have outperformed the stock market by a factor of 15! An organization or a business is built through its people. And what more effective way to build an organization than to create a culture that perpetuates growth, development and excellence?

PROGRESSIVE HUMAN RESOURCE STRATEGIES

A collaborative study conducted by author-consultant-educator Rosabeth Moss Kanter appeared in her book, *The Change Masters.* She compared the long-term financial performance of forty-seven companies, described as progressive, with a similar number of nonprogressive companies. "Progressive" is defined as having progressive human-resource strategies. Well, no surprise there. During a twenty-five-year period, the progressive companies "were significantly higher in long-term profitability and financial growth than their counterparts."

THE EFFECTIVE CULTURE

The culture of any company is its personality. Just as an individual's personality reflects his or her inner character, the same is true of an organization. The organization's personality—the culture—is created by many individuals, but principally by the CEO and the senior-management team. Within a company's culture are the deeply held attitudes that form the work ethic. From this process comes a corporate disposition or attitude that affects how capable the manpower is to facilitate change. If investment in the growth and development of the people in an organization has been made, then the health of the enterprise bodes well for the future. It seems so obvious. In fact, it is basic common sense, but, unfortunately, not common practice.

Nothing stays the same. Everything in the universe either is growing or decaying. As soon as a tree has been cut, the process of decay begins. The process occurs in several phases—from raw timber, to structure, to the razed building, then to the scrap heap. Whether slow or fast, the process of decay has begun. There is a parallel for humanity—both physically and intellectually.

—— ◇ ——

If we are not moving ahead through learning, then we risk being overtaken by those who are.

—— ◇ ——

To stand still is to decline. In order to resist decline, some effort must be exerted. Prior knowledge eventually becomes passé. Both individuals and businesses must constantly be in the process of renewal-through-learning in order to achieve their goals.

It is the responsibility of management to create a culture in which opportunity and personal growth are emphasized if the company itself expects to achieve growth.

PEOPLE ARE THE PROCESS

Where change has dealt an unfriendly or unexpected hand to a business, and the business has played it effectively, it is because of the people in the organization. They were prepared. Although they may have been taken by surprise, they nevertheless had been acculturated to deal with it. People *are* the process. The *right* people, properly prepared, comprise the *right* strategy for meeting change and putting it to work for the company.

A STRATEGY FOR CHANGE

In the next chapter, we examine the role of strategy in business. But first, I want to look specifically at how strategy relates to change. Strategic processes, those things businesses do to implement strategy, are created with the future in mind. In developing strategies, one begins with the end in mind by asking the question: What result is sought? Once that is known, steps can be developed to deliver the desired outcomes.

It is this type of strategic thinking that implicitly raises the question: What must we do to effectively meet the demands of change? As noted above, having your people prepared for change is a critical strategy because they, in turn, will determine what the business needs to do in order to be prepared for change.

As a CEO, I have led the annual strategic planning processes for several businesses. This is an invaluable process for preparing to meet the future. The quality with which analysis and planning is carried out is in direct proportion to the background, training and qualifications of those involved in the process. Quite simply, the best solution is preparation—a well-conceived, people-development strategy that is comprehensively designed and mentored to prepare the organization to function at peak performance.

STRATEGIC MENTORING

As mentioned in Chapter One, I have found mentoring to be the most effective means to support the processes necessary to develop and keep an organization intellectually healthy and fit—prepared to deal with change. Increasingly, we are in the knowledge business. Just keeping up with the knowledge explosion in business, even with a focused, disciplined effort, is daunting. Any company that does not have a strategy in place to meet this business challenge is absolutely flirting with disaster.

The answer lies in facilitating, guiding and encouraging perpetual innovation, learning, and growth. It must be targeted at all levels, strategically aimed at developing the culture, the work groups, and the individuals. This is how you prepare to meet change.

This is not to say that just implementing a strategy is the answer. Absolutely not. But this is the place to start. And it's a long trip. One that really never ends. In the next chapter we will look at strategy in a much broader context, yet still with significant emphasis on people development.

MENTOR'S CHECKUP

◇ What change strategies have you considered?

◇ What is the most serious threat to your business over the next two-to-five years?

◇ Who is working on the measures to effectively deal with change?

◇ To what extent is the business' senior management group involved in preparing to meet the future?

◇ In that regard, what is being done this week?

CHAPTER THREE

STRATEGY MAKES THE DIFFERENCE

OVERVIEW

While the creation of a successful future for one's business is of increasing concern to many managers, it ought to be a compelling concern to all. Just take a look at the number of current business publications focusing on success and you get an idea of the breadth of the issue. And the depth of interest. Despite this appetite for success, many businesses are "going hungry" because there are no easy answers. Change is creating greater unpredictability in the marketplace. As a result, traditional management strategies no longer assure a high probability of success. In response to the rapid change occurring in the general business environment, individual companies need to design management strategies that will remain dynamic.

Strategic mentoring is the way for a company to build a successful future. Since a comprehensive mentoring process is fundamentally based in strategy, a consideration of the practical applications of strategy must be developed. Strategic thinking is essential to the business and to mentoring. Understanding the role and importance of strategy is integral to developing an appreciation for the potential value of a comprehensive mentoring strategy.

MUCH ADO ABOUT STRATEGY

A stroll through the business section of your favorite bookstore will reveal that strategic planning has been a hot topic the past few years. Whenever I meet with fellow CEOs, conversations often turn to discussions of strategy.

IMPLEMENTATION OPPORTUNITIES

With so much attention focused on the subject of strategy by writers, consultants, and educators, I have to wonder where the audience is. If the books are being read, the consulting engagements are being undertaken and the students actually are absorbing this information, then we still have lots of work to do in the area of implementation. All the indicators, whether business journals, conference discussions, business relationships or personal experiences, point to how much work needs to be done to actually implement these processes. Numerous strategies are available to us. The challenge is in their application and implementation.

MESSAGE FROM THE COMPETITORS

The desire to improve results in American business has received a lot of press attention over the past few years. Particularly in light of some of the spectacular results achieved by our international competitors. It has been made pretty clear that the U.S. has been outthought by a number of our international competitors. This tells me the strategies that were in place here in the U.S. were deficient. Otherwise, the results in automobile manufacturing, electronic merchandising and steel manufacturing, to name a few big business categories, would have been different. Of course, hindsight makes it an easy call. But history is a valuable educator. Let's look at what may have been missing.

WHAT IS STRATEGY?

Essentially, strategy consists of the processes and guidelines necessary to achieve an objective or objectives. I define strategic planning as a comprehensive process, involving all levels of management, that anticipates and guides the future or an organization. The CEO is critical to the success of this process and must provide the vision and drive to make it a cultural imperative within the organization. The CEO leads the senior management team through the process of determining, on behalf of the corporation:

◇ Where we are right now

◇ How we got here

◇ Where we want to go and why

◇ How we will get there

◇ Who is responsible for what

◇ When it should be done

The information developed through this exercise enables the management team to make timely, strategic decisions that help set the direction of the business.

Having the management team go through this exercise is a good first step. To develop a continuous strategic planning process that keeps getting better—and that keeps providing better direction—requires intense commitment and focus. Probably the best way to develop an understanding of strategy and strategic planning is to consider the necessary characteristics of the process.

◇ *Continuous and Dynamic*—Strategic planning is a continuous process. It has to be sensitive to market conditions, providing valuable opportunities to feed in new information and making adjustments based on new data to enhance the business results. It also needs to be long-term oriented.

◇ *Analytical and Introspective*—Partial information can be a real threat to strategic planning. Paralysis by analysis can be an obstacle as well. A balanced approach to gaining knowledge about the market dynamics, through processes similar to SWOT (strengths, weaknesses, opportunities, threats) analyses is essential. Also, existing activities need to be examined regularly for their contribution to the business strategy.

◇ *Creative*—Looking at the business and its resources with the goal of maximizing performance and results is a creative process. The best intuition and judgment from the management team is needed.

The core business competencies of the people need to be examined so that human resource growth strategies can be implemented where needed to support continued peak performance.

◇ *Action Oriented*—Ultimately the strategic plan calls for specific action. On a priority basis, it addresses the way in which the resources of the business are best used and when, where, how and by whom. The "why" is the driving force behind the allocation.

◇ *Customer Oriented*—How well we meet the customer's needs and expectations is integral to how successful we are in achieving our business objectives. Strategic planning must include feedback mechanisms to help measure whether we're making a difference with the customer.

◇ *Focused*—Strategic planning is a comprehensive process that involves all aspects of the business' operations. In order for the plan to work, all major decisions must be made with reference to the plan. To do otherwise could seriously dilute the impact of the strategic process and the business results. Discipline is essential.

◇ *Change Oriented*—Without a process to facilitate change, your business is at the mercy of fragmented decision-making. Strategic planning offers a comprehensive means of factoring in the anticipated effects of change and to plan and react in a studied way

—— ◇ ——

The spirit of a team working in harmony can create a powerful force for excellence.

—— ◇ ——

HOW IS STRATEGY APPLIED?

First, let's look at three different forms of business strategy and what is distinctive in their applications. These three forms are quite broad but they highlight the major differences in the application of strategic thinking.

ENTREPRENEURIAL

A number of writers have identified the strategic phenomenon often used by entrepreneurs—"Ready, Fire, Aim." It's absolutely amazing how many times it has worked! Some of my entrepreneurial colleagues have even commented to me, with some pride, how well this approach has worked for them. Let's face it—there must be something else at play. And there is. Entrepreneurs are usually gifted with insight, intuition, unconscious clarity, vision and drive. They usually produce very good results the first time. But if they don't, they are quick to realize something isn't working and to make corrections—quickly. At least the successful ones do. I believe that's one of their "secrets"—responsiveness.

In smaller, entrepreneur-driven businesses, this approach to "strategic planning" can and usually does work. The question is: For how long? The entrepreneur is in charge of both strategic planning and its implementation. Hands-on involvement is the usual hallmark of such management because it facilitates quick responses when needed. So, this one-person approach to strategic planning can work with small businesses. But the business can grow so fast that it outstrips the entrepreneur's ability to cope with the increased challenges to make course corrections quickly.

MID-MARKET COMPANIES

I have spent most of my career in mid-market-sized companies. Usually such companies are in transition because they have outdistanced the entrepreneurial management mode and are en route to building a management team that will enable them to continue to grow.

I define mid-market companies as those which are not publicly traded and which have annual revenues between $15 and $300 million. Management can still make decisions and implement them quickly, but it is done by a team of senior managers rather than an individual. Strategic development is recognized as a crucial part of the chief executive's responsibility, which usually takes the form of a management-team effort led by the CEO. In fact, it should be CEO-driven. To be truly effective, strategic development requires the CEO's enthusiastic leadership. Under the CEO's guidance, senior management must be intimately involved in its formulation and execution.

In the entrepreneurial setting, as soon as the entrepreneur notices that his or her strategy isn't working, changes in strategic direction can be, and usually are, made. The same is true, or should be, in the mid-sized business environment. It is important that the senior management team be involved in regular course-evaluation-

and-adjustment processes. It's the kind of dynamic that the entrepreneur can execute in walkabout sessions, but which later becomes more of a review and analysis process as the business grows. To have only one person responsible for the process becomes increasingly difficult, if not impossible. Executing significant course corrections on a timely basis is best handled as a team function.

———— ◇ ————

For future competitiveness in an increasingly knowledge-driven environment, the big winners are going to be the ones who can perform with agility, making course corrections quickly.

———— ◇ ————

BIG BUSINESS (USUALLY PUBLICLY TRADED)

Most big businesses know the importance of operating strategically. Or at least the senior managers do. What is missing in the problem cases is the involvement of knowledgeable participant-leaders in the execution process, persons who can quickly bring about a critical course correction. Big businesses can easily get too bureaucratic and often may require seven managers, three vice presidents and the CEO, COO or CFO to approve a critical change.

Hey, I've been there and I understand the need for control. My point here, though, is that for future competitiveness in an increasingly knowledge-driven environment, the big winners are going to be the ones who can perform with agility, making course corrections quickly, whether the business is at the entrepreneur, mid-size, or big-business stage.

FLEXIBLE AND DYNAMIC STRATEGY

The strategic planning process in the real world of business change must be flexible. Often, the strategy must be adjusted in response to the requirements and opportunities of the moment.

—— ◇ ——

Opportunities come up that were unknown or even unneeded at the time of planning, requiring a planning process capable of quick adjustments based on the new knowledge.

—— ◇ ——

The introduction of Honda motorcycles into the U.S. market in the late 1950s is a good example of this process. Honda's intended strategy was to market sturdy, well-built, road-worthy 250cc and 305cc motorcycles. That strategy was threatened by product reliability issues. Interestingly, Honda executives were using little 50cc motorbikes to run a lot of their errands around Los Angeles, where their headquarters were located. These Honda 50s attracted a lot of attention. In particular, Sears came up with the strategy of selling the Honda 50s nationwide to a different market—those who really did not consider themselves motorcyclists. To make a long story short, an unanticipated opportunity emerged that launched the Honda motorcycle success. By 1964 nearly one out of every two motorcycles sold in the U.S. was a Honda. The point? Be on the lookout for unexpected opportunities! The best resource for doing this, especially in this knowledge-driven age, is a team of empowered leaders involved in continuous learning.

——— ◇ ———

A comprehensive mentoring strategy
can help develop the culture for spotting and
exploiting opportunities.

——— ◇ ———

A STRATEGY-DRIVEN BUSINESS GETS *PREFERRED* RESULTS

In the process of looking for the most potentially successful business strategies, I have read hundreds of business books, not unlike many other CEOs and senior managers who either have responsibility for running, or ownership in a company. We want state-of-the-art ideas on how to achieve success in the contemporary environment.

The best information indicates that the chances of achieving success are highest when these parameters are present:

◇ *Superior Performance*—We want our companies to obtain the best performance we can muster from our human resources. The objective is to achieve results that make our board, our employees and the competition stand up and take notice. We need the kind of performance that makes us the leaders in our fields.

◇ *Improved Quality*—In order to meet the demands of next week, next month and next year, our quality must constantly be scrutinized to make sure we remain competitive. Therefore, quality must always be improving. As a result, improved quality is a process we want our colleagues focused on as well. To remain a world-class competitor, ongoing quality surveillance and tweaking is required at all levels.

◇ *Customer Service with "WOW"*—So much has been written about exceptional customer service. Yes, most everyone knows how Nordstrom's did it, but I want to know how I can infuse that kind of ethos into my own company.

◇ *Energized Work Force*–To achieve the kind of success that we all want, our colleagues need to show up on Monday mornings, enthusiastic and ready to do business. We would love for them to be pushing their way through the corridors just to get to their desks to get started. We have read about the wonderful organizations where employees embody these qualities. But how do *we* get there?

◇ *Fulfillment and "Funfillment"*–To create the kind of organization that can deliver superior performance, not only must there be fulfillment of the individuals, but "funfillment" along the way as well. Having fun on the job just seems to be a special ingredient to get people to want to show up each day and each week and give it their best shot. I'm not suggesting a continuous party, but rather an informal atmosphere conducive to humor whenever possible. It's a good catalyst for relationship-building.

◇ *Superior Financial Results*-We all want financial success. And just because I've mentioned financial results last doesn't diminish its importance. In fact, this is one of the more important items—the business must be financially successful to continue to grow and invest in its people. We are entitled to a reasonable profit. And all those who make it possible should reap the benefits as well. Therefore, to reap the rewards of performance, quality, etcetera, it is important to emphasize incentives and rewards both on a personal and a corporate level.

A FUTURIST'S PERSPECTIVE

FUTURISTIC THINKING

Since strategy deals with the future, a look at futuristic thinking seems appropriate. Several years ago, I had a most pleasant chance meeting with a gentleman named Glenn Hiemstra, who identified himself as a "futurist." We shared a taxi from Disneyland in Orange County, California to Los Angeles International Airport. I had been taking a couple days off to spend with my family, including my grandchildren, as they discovered that wonderful theme park. My newfound futurist colleague had been involved in a conference at the Disneyland Hotel. Standing in front of the hotel we discovered that we both were heading for the same airport, so we decided to share a taxi.

During the ride, Glenn described how he stimulates people to think about the future. He suggested that we need to consider the three P's of the future—what is *probable, possible* or *preferred*. Later, he sent me his video, which helped me better understand this process. As a business strategist, I quickly adopted this information for use as part of my own evaluative processes. I now understand that if we do not take charge of our opportunities, then most likely we will only achieve what is *probable*. But if we know what is *possible* and can evaluate and strategically plan what we wish to achieve, then we can move toward the *preferred* results. This has become an integral part of my management material— encouraging my colleagues to think in terms of *preferred* results. Our strategies should always reflect that process.

—— ◊ ——

We need to consider the three p's of the future—what is *probable, possible* or *preferred*.

—— ◊ ——

MANAGEMENT'S RESPONSIBILITY

Essentially, management is responsible for obtaining the best possible results—the *preferred results*. Preferred results are derived from a specific, studied process. Our results in the business world are achieved through people. If we can create a process that somehow challenges our main resource—people—to always be growing and looking for ways to improve their performances, then we have released a valuable and powerful force. Creating growth strategies as a part of the company culture also involves developing an understanding of the choices we have and the results we target. The concept of *preferred* results has application for everyone throughout the business. The challenge is to make it part of the organization's culture in order to receive maximum benefits.

EQUIPPING THE TEAM

Directing the business resources toward obtaining preferred results has been my job as CEO. As I look at the various resources with which I have to work, I also apply this thinking to my management colleagues. If the company is to obtain preferred results, then each member of the management team must be prepared to obtain them. Encouraging members of the team to acquire the necessary knowledge skills for better results too often is overlooked as a corporate strategy. A comprehensive mentoring strategy can be the facilitator. Let's now consider the importance of knowledge to business.

KNOWLEDGE MAKES THE DIFFERENCE

Thus far I have been developing a thought process that indicates:

◇ Change is happening at an increasing rate.

◇ Business success requires the right strategy to deal with change.

◇ There are definite performance patterns, whether superior or inferior.

◇ Attaining preferred results requires strategy.

I invite you to consider the role that knowledge plays in an emerging strategy for achieving preferred results. (This will all come together in the next chapter as part of a Strategic Mentoring Model.)

DEMING'S "PROFOUND KNOWLEDGE"

Dr. W. Edwards Deming did much to raise our appreciation of knowledge. His contribution to improved business results is legendary. If you have not read his book, *Out of Crisis,* or Mary Walton's book, *The Deming Management Method,* I commend them to you. Managers need this knowledge, which Deming condensed into fourteen essential points. He referred to them as *profound knowledge.* Having profound knowledge and then applying it increases the probability of achieving preferred results. Central to this process is the improvement (development) of the individual through the acquisition and use of this knowledge.

ESSENTIAL KNOWLEDGE—A QUICK STORY

I recently spent three-and-one-half enjoyable years living in England. The cultural experience was fantastic. During my residence there, I visited London numerous times. I am still in awe of the efficiency and quality of the London taxi service. To satisfy my curiosity, I inquired about the requirements for becoming a taxi driver. Those folks seemed to have memorized all the street patterns, which, if you have visited London, you know are extremely complex. Indeed, I discovered that that is exactly what they must do in order to become taxi drivers. They must acquire a body of *essential knowledge.* In fact, the average London taxi driver candidate makes several attempts over a four-year period before proving he has acquired the essential knowledge to earn a license. Acquisition of this essential knowledge is not the result of an institutionalized process, but, rather, the personal responsibility of each driver. While there are private training programs and coaches available to help the candidates through the process, it is their personal responsibility to become knowledgable enough to pass the exam.

CREATING THE KNOWLEDGE CULTURE

This is a great example for the management environment. Just think what would happen if we could get our colleagues as committed to learning essential knowledge as the London taxi drivers. Conversely, if our management colleagues do not possess knowledge critical to their positions in business, they will be much less effective than they could be. Their lack of knowledge may not be as immediately obvious as it would be with a London taxi driver. Yet the analogy is relevant: Just as the taxi driver would delay the arrival of his passenger at his preferred destination, making the ride more costly; in business, lack of knowledge also will delay, prevent or make it more costly to reach our destination. Without the proper knowledge, it becomes difficult or impossible to obtain preferred results, whether driving a taxi or running a business.

To the extent that we, as managers, can create a process similar to what a London taxi driver must go through to gain essential knowledge for his job, we, too, will benefit. This is the challenge for management: How can we effectively support and encourage our business colleagues to focus on growing their own body of knowledge—their essential and profound knowledge? We want to encourage and support them in the process of becoming the masters of their own qualification processes.

THE ENABLER OF PREFERRED RESULTS—MENTORING

The key to exceptional performance lies in the business culture. How do we achieve these processes that will give us preferred results? What strategies need to be developed to increase the likelihood that preferred results will be realized on a continuous basis? The material in the next chapter focuses on the processes that I believe are necessary for delivering the kinds of results we all really want to see in our organizations. Essentially, it is accomplished through a comprehensive mentoring strategy, driven by the CEO and the senior management team.

——— ◇ ———

The key to exceptional performance lies in the business culture.

——— ◇ ———

The CEO, the business owners and the stockholders all are interested in perpetuating predictable business performance that leads to *preferred* results. Some companies achieve this level of performance every year. A close look at companies that consistently post preferred results reveals a healthy performance strategy. The following chapter introduces and examines mentoring as the specific strategy to create the kind of organization that is capable of producing, executing and realizing excellent business results. The strategy also creates a human resource capable of renewing itself on a continuous basis, one prepared to successfully take the business into the future.

MENTOR'S CHECKUP

◇ How often do you examine your company's strategies? Can they produce preferred results?

◇ When major business decisions are made, do you assess their impact on the strategic plan? On other resources?

◇ How well trained is your senior management staff in the intricacies of strategic planning? Would your results improve if their knowledge increased? How?

◇ What process is in place to ensure that unforeseen opportunities can and will be recognized?

◇ Who are your leaders of tomorrow? Will they be able to perpetuate the business with a high degree of predictability?

CHAPTER FOUR

MENTORING– A SPECIFIC STRATEGY

OVERVIEW

As stated earlier, the coming crisis in business is this: Change is outpacing knowledge. Change also is outpacing the ability of many organizations to do bubble-up analysis and top-down strategy—it just takes too long. As reliance on knowledge and knowledge workers increases, so must the commitment to facilitating learning. An empowered workforce will need to be able to adjust strategies "in the field" in order to seize unanticipated opportunities. Will this create chaos? No, not if it is executed by trained management teams who understand how to function effectively in their environment.

I just spent a couple of days with a good friend of mine who heads a prominent architectural firm. His business grew more than sixty percent last year in an area where other architectural firms were reducing their staff. I spent a day meeting with his partners, helping them examine their strengths, weaknesses, opportunities and threats. An old, familiar pattern was observed. Major investments were being made in technology; little was being done to develop the staff to handle the resulting growth. That's why we were meeting. My friend was seeking "greatness" for his firm and knew that an important element was missing—management and leadership development.

The successful business of the future will have in place a comprehensive strategy to develop its human resources to meet the expanding demands of the marketplace. In the following material, the Strategic Mentoring Model identifies the critical steps necessary to prepare the workforce to successfully meet the future—and progressively guides you through them. Finally, I describe how a systematic approach to analyzing exceptional performance revealed to me the Six Principles for Exceptional Performance.

———— ◇ ————

The successful business of the future will have in place a comprehensive strategy to develop its human resources.

———— ◇ ————

These six principles became apparent as I saw a pattern developing in the transition from poor performance to exceptional performance. This enabled me to identify what I am convinced are the qualities that must be present in order to produce exceptional performance. The next step was to develop a way to replicate those conditions in other business settings. As a result, an implementation strategy emerged, based on the mentoring of performance-enhancing behaviors.

SUCCESSFUL SOLUTIONS

Performance that delivers exceptional results is gratifying, particularly when it is within your own organization. Developing the processes that facilitate exceptional results is senior management's greatest opportunity.

When I speak about "exceptional performance" and "exceptional results," I mean something truly exceeding normal expectations. For example, I recall the truly exceptional performances of Topol in "Fiddler On the Roof," which my wife and I have had the privilege of seeing twice. He received standing ovations both times. In business, I liken this to meeting your banker after a year of exceptional performance and discovering that your personal guarantee is no longer a bank requirement.

Generally, my CEO assignments have been with entrepreneurial organizations. My arrival usually triggered the transitioning from an entrepreneurial-management approach to a team-oriented model. That kind of change usually requires development of new skills, with a particular emphasis on systems improvement.

On one occasion when I was recruited as CEO following an entrepreneur predecessor, I must have found seven project managers, in addition to eight line managers, who had been reporting directly to the entrepreneur. He had been personally managing each relationship and each manager's work performance, including essentially all the decision-making. It was no wonder this entrepreneur was on the verge of collapse. As my management team and I transitioned the business to a systems-oriented, team-management emphasis, a pattern developed. I had seen such a pattern before, but had not taken the time to really understand it.

As so often happens with CEOs, their preoccupation with the trees overrides their attention to what is going on in the forest. Entrepreneurs live in the details, which is where most of their expertise was developed. Although that's what contributes significantly to their success in the developmental stages of the business, there comes a time when the business requires more. And that is when process-focused orientation needs to come into play. Repetitive functions need to be systematized.

———— ◇ ————

**Good systems aid predictability,
and when predictability is achieved,
the enterprise is under stable management.**

———— ◇ ————

SYSTEMS PERSPECTIVE

A systems-oriented approach to management places the emphasis on identifying the specific steps in a process; that is, the individual elements of which it is comprised. This enables the observer to better understand how results are created. Although this is a slight oversimplification, it serves as segue to our next point.

SYSTEMS COMPONENTS

When exceptional performance occurs, I want to understand what was present: What was being done correctly or even exceptionally? What were the "system components"? Was there something extra-special that came into play? A close look at the various elements is helpful in spotting either an aberration or an emerging, new phenomenon. Another reason for the close look is to make sure the individuals or groups get recognition for exceptional performance, which you definitely want to reinforce. Recognition, in turn, encourages more exceptional performance.

In the process of managing several businesses that were undergoing significant change, I discovered the principles necessary for exceptional performance. These principles must be practiced by those creating the business results; i.e., the work force, in order for a company to achieve exceptional performance. That's not to say exceptional performance cannot occur without all of these principles in place; indeed, it is likely that many instances of excellent performance have occurred without these principles. But I'm approaching the problem from a slightly different perspective. First, because I have taken over management of businesses where performance had not been exceptional, I have spent considerable time looking for ways and means to obtain better results. Next, there's the matter of sustaining exceptional performance. What is required is a continuous process, whether making improvements or sustaining high performance. Here is a closer look at the principles.

The Six Principles, taken one at a time, seem so obvious they may provoke a "So what?" response. Their apparent simplicity can be misleading. Although each principle taken alone makes a specific contribution, it is the synergistic, dynamic effect of the combined elements that creates a powerful performance system. It is the relationship among the principles that magnifies their impact on performance behaviors.

SIX PRINCIPLES FOR EXCEPTIONAL PERFORMANCE

1. Knowledge is power; hence, grow knowledge.
2. Leaders create results; hence, develop more leaders.
3. A state of harmony within the organization can more effectively release the full talent of individuals; hence, build harmonious relationships.

4. All development is self-development; hence, facilitate individual growth.

5. Knowledge workers work in small groups; hence, facilitate enhanced group-dynamic skills.

6. The organization's culture creates attitudes for excellence; hence, develop the culture.

DYNAMIC COMPLEXITY

Peter Senge (*The Fifth Discipline*) propounds a concept of *dynamic complexity* that helps explain these relationships. This concept describes situations where cause and effect are subtle, and where the effects over time may not be obvious. The essence of the discipline of "systems thinking" is in seeing processes of change rather than linear cause-and-effect relationships. Instead of noting individual parts, systems thinking takes in the whole picture, the *process.* The process of change, involving the Six Principles, creates a force for excellence like none other I have experienced. Let's take a closer look at what the application of the Six Principles creates.

PERFORMANCE FOCUS

The Six Principles for Exceptional Performance can be divided into two sets of three principles, all with a common focus. Three are based on the "what" (1, 2 and 3) and three on the "who" (4, 5 and 6); that is, *what* needs to be done and *who* should do it:

The *What*	The *Who*
1. Learning	4. Individual
2. Leading	5. Group/team
3. Relating	6. Organization

The *What:* Knowledge and learning processes are evident as an ongoing and highly valued activity. People are taking responsibility, seizing opportunities and observing their achievements.

The *Who:* The people are effective as individuals, in groups or teams; through its culture the organization creates an environment that encourages excellence.

These are the performance drivers. But how are they directed? Does it just happen or is there a grand strategy behind it? The likelihood of improved performance is directly proportional to the quality and depth of implementation.

First, let's look at the relationship between the individual and the processes of learning, leading and relating. This is the path to creating a company staffed with empowered individuals who work effectively together, whether individually, in small or large groups, or as an entire organization.

PERFORMANCE DEVELOPMENT GRID

	Learning	Leading	Relating
Individual	Facilitate continuous individual learning	Facilitate continuous leadership development	Facilitate developing individual relationship building skills
Group/ Team	Facilitate continuous learning about building team excellence	Facilitate team leadership development	Facilitate developing team relationship building skills
Organization	Facilitate the development of a learning organization	Facilitate the development of leadership at all levels	Facilitate a culture that emphasizes positive working relationships

TABLE 4-1

Above we have a visual model of the "critical knowledge" that exceptional performers need to have on the one axis, and the people application on the other axis. (See discussion in Chapter Three on critical knowledge.) And that brings us to the master process that makes all of this work—*Mentoring*.

MENTORING FOCUS—GROWTH AND RENEWAL

Mentoring was defined in Chapter One, but for the sake of continuity in our logical development of the mentoring model, let's review. Your objective is to assist your business colleagues in the process of growth and renewal, which means that they need to make the critical knowledge described above their own. We know our workers, who increasingly are becoming "knowledge workers," are going to be more prepared to meet future work demands if they are involved in developing their "critical knowledge." You want them to be developed and empowered to produce exceptional results.

FACILITATE DEVELOPMENT

Personal development cannot be mandated. Since all human resource development begins with self-development, management can most effectively serve as facilitator and motivator. And with knowledge workers, my experience has been that mentoring is the most effective process to facilitate development.

There always will be the odd individual, maybe even several, who will not take advantage of a growth opportunity. I recall one of these unusual occasions a few years ago. I was going to lead a book discussion group for a team of junior managers in my company's finance department. Doing this several times a year throughout a company has given me an excellent opportunity to model, communicate and encourage continuous learning. By facilitating it, I demonstrate that I practice the principles I espouse. There are other desirable benefits as well, such as team building, relationship building, and culture building. In any event, one young woman asked to speak to me about the book discussion session. She reported that her husband felt that if she was going to participate in this type of activity, then she should also be given the opportunity to read the book on company time. He didn't think it was fair for her to have to use her personal time outside of work for business-related reading. I was encountering a classic, and common, case of not understanding the concept of personal responsibility for personal growth. Our conversation went something like this (we'll call her Sue):

HJ: Oh, I realize it must be difficult for working couples to find time to do all the things that need to be done outside of working hours. It's not easy. Is this book discussion group activity something you really want to do? (It was a brown bag lunch session on the lunch hour, plus up to another hour of company time—so no home time lost).

Sue: Yes, I think so. But George, my husband, gets very concerned if I have to use my personal time for something related to work.

HJ: Yes, I think I understand. Let me ask you a couple of questions. Do you very much enjoy reading or watching TV?

Sue: I don't get to do much reading because George likes me to watch television with him most evenings. That is, after the dishes are done and the like.

HJ: I see. So it may be a time problem for you, since you seem to have most of your home time allocated, right?

Sue: Yes, I guess so.

HJ: First, Sue, let me explain what I think we are trying to accomplish with our book discussion group, and let's see if it makes sense, okay?

Sue: Sure.

HJ: The book discussion group meeting is a purely optional activity. It's something we started doing several years ago when three young managers asked me if I could recommend a good business book for them to read. They felt, because they were fairly new managers, that acquiring some additional information might help them become more effective in their jobs. Well, I was delighted. You see, everyone really has to be responsible for their own personal growth. No one knows better than that individual what particular growth may be needed. Also, learning takes personal commitment. It has to be something a person wants to do. But when anyone in our company shows real interest in gaining knowledge, I want to support that effort. That's because people involved in learning are growing and preparing themselves for the future, and hopefully, for bigger and better jobs. The truth is that we all win because the company also needs people who are ready to be promoted when the opportunity arises. Does that make sense?

Sue: Oh yes, it sure does.

HJ: I was just thinking, if you would really like to see if being involved in a personal growth activity is rewarding to you, how about coming in to work a little earlier, or using your lunch hour, or any other free time you can create to do some of your reading of the book. Give it a try and see if it is something you see real value in. Look at it as a personal investment, one that only you can make. See if there is some personal benefit or enjoyment you get out of the process. I must admit I have a bit of a bias about these kinds of activities. I think people really do get more out of it when they make a personal investment. It's their own future they are preparing for and investing in. It just seems to be taken more seriously when personal time and commitment are involved. What do you think?

Sue: Yes, I would like to give it a try. I think I can probably do most of my reading on my lunch hour. Thank you.

Well, Sue did attend the book discussion meeting. And she participated in the discussions. I believe I was able to help her shift to a new view of learning at a personal level. This type of scenario has recurred with other "Sues," each somewhat different, but usually their reluctance is related to the time requirement involved.

WHAT TO MENTOR

What kind of knowledge do mentors need to facilitate? I have identified the critical knowledge of learning, leading and relating. This is quite general and needs to be tailored to fit the circumstances in each environment. But generally, the following should be considered:

◇ *Learning*–We need to support and facilitate the acquisition of knowledge in general, but particularly of business fundamentals. A well-educated, well-trained and intellectually stimulated work force is the basis of a strategy for meeting the business demands of the future. A widespread emphasis on learning can have an invigorating effect on a company's culture. A company that is actively pursuing the growth of knowledge, both individually and corporately, creates an invigorating dynamic. Learning-oriented people will be attracted as well. (Specific material is presented in Chapter Nine about mentoring a learning organization.) Learning should be a major element of a company's culture, one which is valued by the CEO and management as a significant opportunity for the people in the company.

◇ *Leading*–The cultivation and development of leaders stimulates decision-making and creates better results. Essentially, what leaders do is take responsibility for results. They see an opportunity and just naturally want to convert it to a beneficial outcome. This is great stuff, particularly when this comes together in the culture with empowered learners. (Material in Chapter Ten presents an in-depth look at the process involved in mentoring leaders while developing vision.) Developing knowledgeable leaders is the best strategy for a successful future.

◇ *Relating*—Relationships hold the organization and the culture together. The people to whom management and leadership responsibilities are entrusted will be more effective with a deepened understanding of human relations skills, diagnostics and practices. This element of the mentoring "package" completes the comprehensive program content for strengthening of the core abilities of future leaders.

—— ◇ ——

A well-educated, well-trained and intellectually stimulated work force is the basis of a strategy for meeting the business demands of the future.

—— ◇ ——

Knowledge, leadership and relationship skills are the skills needed to lead tomorrow's organizations. (Chapter Eleven contains essential information on the importance of relationship-building skills.) Focusing on relationships often requires that the manager-leader deal with behavioral issues. Chapter Fifteen provides insights for dealing with behavioral matters. Together, the material provides guidelines for mentoring growth and development in these important areas.

WHOM TO MENTOR

The basic content of a comprehensive mentoring strategy has now been described. The next consideration is who should be on the receiving end of this process? Who should be mentored? Implementing the mentoring process focuses on three "Whos"—the individual, the groups, and the organization as a whole. Each requires a unique strategy.

◇ *Individual*–This is the basic building block of a mentoring program, since all development starts with individuals. Chapter Six contains specific guidelines and content for an effective individual mentoring program. Chapters Twelve and Thirteen present specific information on the responsibilities and roles of both the mentor and the mentee. This one-on-one relationship between mentor and mentee potentially creates an enormous growth opportunity for the mentee. Knowing how to guide it in a productive manner is the challenge to every mentor. So, even the mentor needs to be developing in order to fulfill his responsibility as an effective mentor. Specific steps and strategies for this process are discussed in these two chapters.

◇ *Groups*–Increasingly, work is being performed by knowledge workers in small group settings. More businesses and segments of businesses are being managed by teams rather than individuals. Small working groups are becoming increasingly more effective in dealing with complex projects or operations due to the variety and depth of knowledge required. When these small groups are cohesive and dynamic, they can function in unity, as a team, and a potential for exceptional performance is present. Mentoring can be effectively applied to small groups to facilitate growth in these areas, which enables more effective performance by the group. As CEO, it has been my aim to mentor my executive team to function as an efficient leadership unit that is stronger and more effective than the sum of the parts. More information is presented on this topic in Chapter Seven.

◇ *Organization*–Mentoring the organization primarily falls under the purview of the chief executive and senior management. The process is achieved by cultivating an atmosphere that supports the mentoring objectives, which are to enhance the three "Whats"–learning, leadership and relationships. Chapter Eight provides an in-depth look at what is involved in building a culture that supports the objectives of the mentoring strategy.

Mentors facilitate, guide and encourage continuous innovation, learning and growth. That's what mentors do, nonstop. It becomes a way of life. Mentors become nonstop. It becomes a way of life. Mentors become conditioned to look for opportunities to facilitate, guide and encourage. Sounds like a good job, right? There's none better. What a fantastic opportunity and an honor, I believe, to be a catalyst in the process of helping people grow and move their careers onto an upward track. Who better than the CEO and his or her senior management team to ensure that the business culture understands and supports this growth strategy?

—— ◇ ——

**Mentors facilitate, guide and encourage
continuous innovation, learning and growth.**

—— ◇ ——

This concludes the overview of mentoring strategy. The Performance Development Grid (Table 4-1) identifies the nine mentoring relationships for which specific strategies will be identified. This model establishes the specifications for a comprehensive mentoring strategy.

STRATEGIC MENTORING MODEL

The objective of the Strategic Mentoring Model (Table 4-2) is to identify the specific strategies that facilitate development of the business' human resources so they can achieve exceptional results. Actual development is carried out by executing the comprehensive mentoring strategy.

—— ◇ ——

**The more elegant the execution,
the more elegant the results.**

—— ◇ ——

There are nine distinct strategies to be executed to realize the full application and benefit of the Strategic

Model. And as indicated in the title of the last chapter, strategy makes the difference. And more than any other strategy, this one has to be driven from the top. This comprehensive strategy will create the future of the enterprise. The more elegant the execution, the more elegant the results. With so much to gain, or lose, one can see the justification for having this comprehensive mentoring strategy under the guidance of the chief executive and top management.

BENEFITS OF THE MENTORING STRATEGY

As managers, we have both the opportunity and the responsibility to provide developmental coaching or counseling to those managers who report to us. Every manager has the duty to equip subordinate managers to be as effective as possible. The more you can prepare your managers to deal with the ever-increasing complexities of business management, the greater the likelihood that you will get the business results you want.

If you are focused on achievement, one of the more frustrating experiences in life is to see potential go unused. This is particularly true for parents. To realize that your children possess gifts they refuse to use is very frustrating. Managers experience this frustration, too, with team members whose potential remains untapped. Mentoring is a strong force for unleashing talent, the underutilized resource.

A resourceful manager-leader constantly looks for ways to improve performance. In today's rapidly changing business environment, the savvy manager is looking for every possible method for achieving greater effectiveness. Let's look at the benefits to the various parties involved: the mentee, the mentor, and the organization.

STRATEGIC MENTORING MODEL

	Learning	Leading	Relating
Individual	**Facilitate continuous individual learning**	**Facilitate individual leadership development**	**Facilitate developing individual relationship-building skills**
	As the basic building block of performance, Individual Learning involves a commitment to self-mastery and a continuous quest for knowledge. As conducting a successful business becomes increasingly knowledge based (knowledge is power), the importance of individual learning is paramount.	Leadership occurs when individuals identify an opportunity to make something positive happen, and then take responsibility for the results. Followership, the essential companion, occurs when the leader offers a trustworthy direction. The best strategy creating followership is to provide a model others will follow.	People create results, and people who work together accomplish even better results. Business usually requires people to work together for results. Therefore, effective people skills are an essential element of today's top business performers.
Group/ Team	**Facilitate continuous learning on building team excellence**	**Facilitate team leadership development**	**Facilitate developing team relationship-building skills**
	The advantage of working groups is the collective knowledge and skills that may be used in achieving a goal. Especially effective is a group that also begins to learn together from sources within and outside the group.	Many successful businesses are led by small teams that may be found at any level within the management hierarchy. Increasing team leadership capabilities helps create even more internal resources that can be used towards achieving good business results.	Groups that work well together have greater opportunity for achieving good results. Group success depends on building member relationships and drawing upon the abilities of all members.
Organization	**Facilitate the development of a learning organization**	**Facilitate the development of leadership at all levels**	**Facilitate a culture that emphasizes positive working relationships**
	Knowledge and information are critical commodities of the future. Future success is much more likely when continuous learning becomes an integral part of the culture of an organization.	Cultivating leadership at all levels is one of the most effective success strategies. Supporting and cultivating leaders to take responsibility will provide the necessary resources for tomorrow's challenges. Leaders should serve as models while carrying out the corporate strategy.	People who work together effectively create better results. Working together effectively requires positive, supportive relationships. The organization's culture establishes the moral and ethical guidelines that create the character of the organization. The successful organization will manifest a culture built on character principles that produce excellence at all levels.

TABLE 4-2

BENEFITS TO THE MENTEE

In both the public and the private sectors, intellectual breakthroughs usually occur beyond the constraints of traditional thinking. I attended a seminar on creativity several years ago in which the leader introduced us to the concept of "getting outside of the nine dots." The objective of the exercise is to connect the nine dots printed in a square pattern with four straight lines without lifting the pen (Figure 4-3).

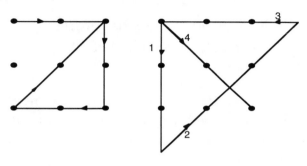

FIGURE 4-3

Somehow our thinking patterns (or paradigms) cause us to assume that we have to stay within the square pattern. But the task becomes quite simple once we realize that by breaking outside of the square pattern we can, indeed, connect the nine dots. The difficulty is in breaking out of the mind-set that compels us to stay within the traditional pattern. That's how I believe the mentoring process works: It takes an exceptional process to create exceptional results.

It was through near desperation that I discovered the benefits of mentoring. As described in Chapter One, I was in the difficult situation of having to provide management leadership in a very challenging environment. I had encountered a particularly knotty problem that exceeded my creative solutions at the time. I began to search for someone who might help me discover the answer. Indeed, I did find a mentor, as I noted earlier.

I firmly believe that my mentoring experience significantly contributed to my career successes. Mentoring helped prepare and develop me to deal with increasingly complex management issues in a much more effective way. I could have groped my way through the management wilderness, as I had earlier, finding answers from various sources.

———— ◇ ————

**It takes an exceptional process
to create exceptional results.**

———— ◇ ————

My mentor served as a guide to the mentee (me), which enabled me to achieve desired results sooner than otherwise would have been possible. The benefits the mentee receives are these:

◇ Direction for personal growth

◇ Clarification regarding career goals and career growth

◇ Reference for problem analysis

◇ Feedback on growth progress

◇ Sourcing of growth information

BENEFITS TO THE MENTOR

Significantly, if the mentor has a stake in the outcome of the business, he contributes to the likelihood of better results. Yet, the process goes far beyond that. Personally, I have found it very gratifying to give something back to the management profession. In addition, mentoring allows me to model the leadership principles that I believe in.

In this process of mentoring, the mentor also achieves personal growth. One needs to give in order to receive. In order for the water in a lake to remain clear and fresh, it needs to have an outlet, to circulate, or it will stagnate, which is an apt metaphor for the human development process. By teaching, one learns. As a mentor, the necessity of remaining current with information and trends in the business environment usually benefits me as much as the mentee.

The mentor also benefits from constantly reviewing previously learned information. Mentoring provides an opportunity to brush up on business concepts that may have become vague or been forgotten with time.

BENEFITS TO THE ORGANIZATION

Just imagine what a comprehensive mentoring program can accomplish when managers are motivated to be the best they can be. When the organization benefits, everyone benefits. I have seen people who were excited just to be a part of the mentoring program. I have also seen people who were not involved in the same mentoring program feel left out of something very special. Getting people excited about their jobs and improving their performance is a manager's dream. A mentoring program can do this, and do it without manipulating or taking advantage of anybody. Some of the tangible benefits to an organization include the following:

◇ Improved communication

◇ Improved leadership

◇ Improved motivation and morale

◇ Improved recruitment

◇ Improved financial performance

◇ Improved work force capabilities

◇ Energized corporate culture

Not many programs can provide that many benefits. Mentoring goes to the heart of what drives an organization: its people and its culture. I have witnessed the high degree of motivation and other positive effects that occur in companies where employees feel that management really cares for them, and wants to see them succeed. The successful mentoring program is the result of a distinct strategy that is well-planned and very well-executed. Sure, even a so-so mentoring program probably is better than nothing. But why not make your mentoring relationship or program the best possible? In one sense, all managers by association are supposed to be mentors, leaders and, now, even coaches. Do they, and you, have a road map to ensure their success, and thus your own?

YOUR STRATEGY

A word of caution. This is not a quick-fix process. Comprehensive and strategic mentoring is a long-term process. A lot of preparation, design and planning are required to tailor a strategy to a particular organization. Most of us have learned that really exceptional results don't come easily. That's what makes such results and the people who produce them so special and elusive. The guidance process necessary to launch a successful mentoring program is presented in the next chapter.

MENTOR'S CHECKUP

◊   How would you describe the condition of your company's basic business systems; that is, the core systems the business depends on every day just to function? Does each system have a "master"?

◊   How many work groups can you identify to which you make a contribution? How would you describe your contribution?

◊   How would you describe the awareness level in your organization regarding the importance of relationships?

◊   Do you know anyone in your organization who currently is being mentored? Can it be expanded? Who's driving it?

◊   How does human-resource development fit into your organization's business strategy?

CHAPTER FIVE

LAUNCHING A MENTORING PROGRAM

OVERVIEW

Deciding to implement a mentoring program is the first step in a series of important steps to strengthen your human resources. A systematic and thoughtful approach at the beginning will increase the likelihood of successful results. Broad-based support and participation from the senior management group is needed from the outset. In fact, participation in the strategy, design and implementation by senior management is essential. Their involvement in modeling and mentoring growth and development is key to its success. While each mentoring program should be tailored to a particular setting, an implementation and maintenance model is presented as a guide.

All development starts with the individual. When an organization becomes committed to a comprehensive mentoring program, the culture will support and encourage personal growth. Self-development and self-mastery figure prominently in the overall strategy for growth and development. A step-by-step implementation model is presented as a guide, starting with ownership and commitment. If the CEO and the senior management team are the models, a mentoring culture that produces exceptional results will follow.

IMPLEMENTATION

I personally have been involved in implementing mentoring and continuous learning processes in several organizations that I have managed. As one would expect, each was unique. There are common principles that serve each, and a cycle of steps to follow (Table 5-1). Generally, these are the steps that worked well for the management team. I present these well-tested principles, which are essential in assessing the culture, the environment and the personnel of organizations, in order to design specific implementational approaches for each particular setting. All of which is to say that a cookie-cutter approach won't work.

1. OWNERSHIP AND COMMITMENT

This is a most important ingredient in the success of your overall mentoring and management development processes. As chief executive, you can provide support, input, urging and admonition, but if you do not provide the opportunity for ownership—participation in design, implementation and management, then the results likely will be "underwhelming." Fortunately, bright, successful people will want to be involved in the developmental aspects. In addition, an individual will identify with the results by having been one of the creators. This adds a liveliness and an energy to the processes that make them even more effective.

STRATEGIC MENTORING MODEL
IMPLEMENTATION AND MAINTENANCE CYCLE

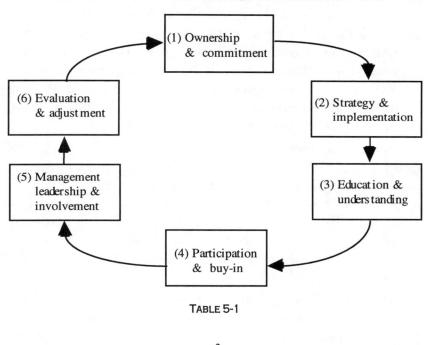

TABLE 5-1

———— ◇ ————

**If you do not provide the opportunity for ownership—
participation in design, implementation
and management—then the results
are likely to be "underwhelming."**

———— ◇ ————

2. STRATEGY AND IMPLEMENTATION

There are many ways in which a mentoring program can be administered and facilitated. Here's a method that's worked for me. Naturally, I consider it to be among the most effective. For maximum impact on the organization, I try to organize the management hierarchy into only three levels: senior management, mid-management and supervisory. Of course, the size of the organization has much to do with structure. Fairly flat organizational structures minimize the levels through which information and leadership direction must be filtered. Such a tri-level structure has worked well for me. In a mentoring organization, flatness facilitates management's direct involvement in the implementation, which makes the job easier and the outcome more successful. In the process, the managers become owners of the results.

Each management level embodies two tracks of development. The first is general learning and knowledge expansion, which includes a reading program, seminar attendance, and the like. Participants are encouraged to become fully involved in the design of the program. Clarity is essential so that real understanding, appreciation and commitment can develop. After that, the program is fleshed out.

The second track, which is more specific, is developed as a core-competency training program. Senior management is responsible for ensuring that training and development are provided in these core skill areas. Each department head is asked to contribute to this process by helping to design the overall management training program for that department. Senior management should evaluate their overall staffing, and assess what types of development will produce a turned-on, energized group of colleagues. The human resources staff also can add value here.

Each member of the management staff also assesses his own development needs. There are many effective self-assessment tools; integrating the right one into a specific business environment is preferable to an "off-the-shelf" approach. After this assessment has been completed, all participants will know where they need to aim their development activities.

Human resources managers should take responsibility for the creation of a core-training module for each of the areas identified in the training program. Such training will have been resourced both internally and externally through a methodical process in which management evaluated the various training options and selected the most appropriate one. One of the core training sessions should explain the company culture and its commitment to continuous learning.

3. EDUCATION AND UNDERSTANDING

Before there can be action, or, in this case, implementation, there needs to be understanding. It is important to begin with senior management. While this may differ from organization to organization, generally those who report to the chief executive should be involved and may include the next reporting level, depending on size and number. Every organization has its core management decision-making group and that's the one that should be involved. For example, my department heads have been directly involved in the process in the companies in which I have implemented this process. Each brought to the process a distinct level of understanding and appreciation for the importance of management development. Communicating to this group their responsibility for management development was not difficult. Bringing the strategy to life was the challenge because most managers had no experience in this area.

So, the first step is to equip the core management group with knowledge and appreciation for the benefits of a management-led management-development program. The strategy comes to life through what I call *manage-*

ment mentoring–the management group that models, facilitates, encourages and supports the development of their subordinates and colleagues in an observable, meaningful way.

4. PARTICIPATION AND BUY-IN

There *absolutely must* be commitment, participation, and yes, real buy-in. Otherwise, the strategy will not be realized. Your senior management team has a serious responsibility to lead by example and to demonstrate the process throughout the company. The extent to which senior managers subscribe to their own personal growth may vary. The very fact that you are working with people who have become senior managers indicates that they already have taken steps to develop the necessary awareness, understanding and abilities. Senior managers generally are fairly supportive and enthusiastic about involvement in this overall process. Creating an energized workforce capable of producing exceptional business results is management's dream. Once the benefits are truly understood, support usually follows.

5. MANAGEMENT LEADERSHIP AND INVOLVEMENT

To the extent that I can, I want my senior management team involved in the actual management development activities. Their involvement demonstrates in a very real way our commitment to process, which, in turn, provides several related benefits. In order for senior managers to participate in the mentoring process, they must already be amenable to learning new information and to their own growth. As they acquire knowledge, they need to share it with those whom they are mentoring. As mentoring role models, they need to "walk their talk" if they are truly going to be effective. Thank goodness that by now they have usually been "switched on" enough to realize this.

Many benefits can be realized from having managers teach, but they must be competent teachers. Some coaching may be required to get a manager's teaching skills up to speed. Some people "have it" and some people don't. Don't ruin a learning and development opportunity by having an ineffective person leading it. You are dealing with sensitive issues here. The process requires care and sensitivity. It has not always been possible to have every manager "turned on" to this process. Some have just not been as excited and committed as I would like, and there will always be a weakest contributor on a team.

———— ◇ ————

Training has as much to do with delivery and technique as with content.

———— ◇ ————

Because training is of such core importance, managers must not be appointed to become trainers solely based on their positions. First, it must be determined whether they really want to participate as a trainer; second, their preparedness must be carefully and sensitively evaluated. As is true for any growth activity, the desire has to come from within and if it doesn't, the results most likely will not be what we want. I have shared with my colleagues the exhilaration I've received from teaching management development courses. While I realize it's not the same type of fun for everyone, I will offer to share these opportunities, with some encouragement, with my colleagues. If they then decide it is something they want to try, I will ask them to prepare material and go through a trial run. They need to know that their objective is to have their "students" give this learning process a very positive evaluation rating. You just don't hand somebody a book and say, "Next week come in and share this information with your colleagues." As in any endeavor, to get the best results, start with effective planning and preparation.

At one company, I hired a consultant who specialized in training the trainers. You may wish to consider this. He really helped create a much keener appreciation for the *process* of effective training. Training has as much to do with delivery and technique as with content. Preparation and training are essential considerations in achieving a quality mentoring program.

There's always the problem that a "prophet in his own country" is not as credible as an outsider. The outsider usually has more credibility than one of the internal managers. However, training by internal managers can still work. I merely point this out as both an option to consider and a potential concern to be addressed. I believe that all senior managers should be capable of leading training sessions, since a major portion of their overall management responsibility is to lead growth and development. And I'm not just speaking of the dissemination of knowledge. I want to see training that develops the understanding and commitment necessary to use the knowledge.

6. EVALUATION AND ADJUSTMENT

Any system implementation process needs to include a review and evaluation phase. The system designers and implementors need to be assured that the new system is delivering the desired results. There are many ways in which such a program can run into difficulties. Some enthusiastic manager may try to speed up the process to get more results sooner. Or another may not provide sufficient leadership to develop fundamental support and buy-in. The designers, participants and administrators of the system will benefit by systematically evaluating what can be done to make the processes even better.

LAUNCHING BEGINS WITH COMMITMENT

Before senior management decides to launch a mentoring program, there needs to be a deep understanding of what is required. Creating and maintaining an ongoing, successful mentoring program, one that has a significant impact on business results, is a very big job. A high level of follow-up and commitment will be required for a successful program.

So, before all else, the question must be asked: Is there a sufficient level of commitment at the outset? This is not a cosmetic morale booster. Care must be given to determine at the outset whether there is absolute resolve for success.

CORPORATE COMMITMENT

One of the most disheartening things that can happen in an organization is for a program initiated by senior management to fizzle. Serious damage to management's credibility is the result and then it becomes very difficult to launch subsequent programs. You can almost hear the troops groan, "Oh boy, here comes another one." And those comments are well-deserved if, in fact, management has not developed the follow-through to sustain programs once they are launched. There has been a tendency in American management to embrace "flavor-of-the-month" management programs. I don't need to enumerate all the dazzling and revolutionary ideas that have competed for management's attention over the past few decades. Management's focus should not be deflected from the business basics. If a new concept can enhance our understanding and use of business fundamentals, then we should pay attention. It is important, however, to make sure the energy and management credibility required to improve the productivity of the business is aimed in the right direction.

PERSONAL COMMITMENT—FROM THE TOP

A mentoring program is like any other system in an organization. Only systems that are implemented masterfully, by properly motivated and highly skilled champions, will survive. Every system needs a champion or it will, in fact, die. Therefore, from the outset, someone must have the responsibility for supporting and monitoring the progress of the mentoring program during the subsequent year at weekly and, later, monthly intervals to ensure that it becomes a vital and dynamic part of the company's culture

———— ◇ ————

**Management's focus should not be deflected
from the business basics.**

———— ◇ ————

Mentoring programs remain meaningful only so long as the CEO and senior executives remain personally committed to their existence. Unless the senior management team is fully committed and deeply involved in the mentoring program, its value definitely will be diminished and, unfortunately, the results that could energize and transform the business just will not be realized.

SUSTAINED COMMITMENT

The first step is to make sure a sustainable commitment is made by the company, which will produce a program with ongoing meaning. All too often, initiatives such as mentoring begin with all the goodwill and enthusiasm that an organization can possibly muster. But soon the novelty wears off, the drudgery begins, commitment slackens and what was an enthusiastic beginning becomes merely a mediocre process. So now when I launch such programs, I meet with my key executives and we formally establish meeting times to evaluate the progress of the program. Putting future assessment meetings on the calendar reinforces the importance of continued monitoring for the success of the program.

———— ◇ ————

**The level of belief and commitment
of the CEO and the senior managers
will be mirrored by the culture.**

———— ◇ ————

Another opportunity for a "commitment check" comes with one-on-one meetings between the CEO and members of the senior management team. I have often asked my colleagues to describe how their mentoring process was going. My job is to get them excited about what it can do for them and the group for which they have responsibility. The level of belief and commitment of the CEO and the senior managers will be mirrored by the culture.

MANAGEMENT RESPONSIBILITY

ORGANIZATIONAL HEALTH MAINTENANCE

Mentoring provides many benefits, but the main purpose of a mentoring program is to prepare the business for the future. Comprehensive mentoring offers the best strategy for dealing with change. Preparing the human resources of the business to meet the demands of the future is the key strategy. Through mentoring, management is communicating both its responsibility for developing the people in the organization and their importance to the company. Helping senior management become believers and practitioners is a crucial step in achieving a successful program.

A good place to begin is with each senior manager individually. First, you need to determine where they are in their own development and what kind of commitment they have made to their ongoing personal growth. As I have moved from one organization to another, I have found varying levels of individual awareness and commitment. Generally, I have found that, like most programs that are good for us, human resource development usually doesn't get the attention it deserves. For many, personal development is in the same category as exercise and diet. We all know we ought to be doing it, but often we don't.

PRIORITIES AND CHOICES

Personal development is a matter of personal choice. In the real world of work and other realities, people feel constantly pressured and driven to achieve meaningful results. Family demographics in the last twenty years have changed significantly, resulting in a significant increase in the number of working couples. This usually means a sharing of responsibilities at home, with many constraints on time that otherwise could be used for each person to focus on personal development. Yet everybody has the same amount of time. Ultimately, it comes down to how effectively we use that time. Human nature is such that often we choose the path of least resistance rather than of most discipline—no matter how high the cause of discipline.

DEVELOPMENT STARTS WITH ME— I'M RESPONSIBLE

I'm a big fan of what Stephen Covey has written about the habits of highly effective people. Coming to grips with managing ourselves is an important step in developing the ability to manage others. That fits right in with our philosophy of personal development, which we believe must start with ourselves. As managers, we cannot help develop others unless we, too, are in the process of gaining knowledge and information. Personal development is the source from which we can guide and encourage others' growth and development.

———— ◇ ————

Coming to grips with managing ourselves is an important step in developing the ability to manage others.

———— ◇ ————

Members of the senior management group must be the encouragers, models and facilitators. If we are not modeling personal development and demonstrating its benefits, then it will be a "tough sell" to those whom we are responsible for leading.

DEVELOPMENT CAN BE FUN

Once you and your senior managers have an understanding and a commitment to your mutual responsibilities for management development, you're ready to launch. Getting to this point, in my experience, usually is the result of a series of one-on-one meetings between the CEO and the senior executives. The CEO has the opportunity to engage his or her management team in a tremendously exciting trip on the road to exceptional performance—to meet the winds of change and soar. Obtaining *preferred* results requires continuous modeling. But hey, this can be exciting. I've seen managers really having fun with self-development and management-development. Committed leadership will facilitate a very enjoyable process. Learning can be fun. In fact, the more fun we can inject into our whole organizational culture, the more people will be motivated to become contributors. As planning and strategy sessions are carried out, a good question is, "What can we do to really make this exciting and effective?"

IMPORTANCE OF STRATEGY

On the other hand, I have had the opportunity to observe some startlingly ineffective attempts at management development. I've seen development decisions made on the basis of what pamphlets and fliers hit the desk that week that seem to have the best marketing and public relations thinking behind them. This is indicative of a reactive mode that displaces a strategic process of planned human resource development. I hasten to add that there are core, or basic, seminars and training programs that provide valuable general knowledge. It may be beneficial to incorporate such training sessions into the overall development strategy. However, we should not respond to a brilliant seminar advertisement as the only basis for participating in such an event. To the contrary, the business will benefit most by management having a proactive development strategy for each individual in the organization and then mentoring the process to facilitate maximum learning.

BEING WINNERS

Success and job satisfaction have taken on a new look. The size of one's office, the number of people supervised or other management perks are not necessarily the measure of happiness at the office anymore. Instead, the greatest management high now comes from being a part of a successful, well-run, growing organization. The organization that knows its mission, has vision, and most important, understands the significance of each person's unique contribution, is on the right path. This has been documented for us by leaders of the "excellence" movement of the 1980s (fostered by best-selling author and business consultant Tom Peters); the "total quality" movement at the end of the 1980s and the beginning of the 1990s (Dr. Deming); and, more recently, the "learning organization" (Peter Senge) and the "re-inventing the organization" (Kanter, Belasco, Hamel, Prahalad, et. al.) movements. People want to be on a winning team. In fact, we all want to be winners. Being a part of a winning team gives us a sense of well-being that invigorates our overall effectiveness.

SUPPORT AND MOTIVATE

So what's the objective? In the beginning, it is to encourage managers to learn on behalf of both themselves and the organization. Mentoring a strategic learning program will prepare your colleagues to respond effectively to the changing environment. This is the classic win/win arrangement. With the mobility of careers from business-to-business, as well as the need to have practiced managers in key slots, management development is at the heart of a successful career and a successful business. So management development is both the objective and, in part, the reward. While development and learning do not assure success, they certainly enhance the probability of achieving and sustaining it, as opposed to the alternative. Part of management's task is to help the culture embrace the concept that self-development is a powerful and rewarding process individually and corporately. The culture should support, even encourage, individuals to take responsibility for their own futures through self-development.

SELF-DEVELOPMENT/SELF-MASTERY

LEARNING

A manager's job is to acquire knowledge on behalf of the organization to enable intelligent execution of responsibilities. The individual manager is in the best position to assess what knowledge is important for effective and successful performance on the job. An organization that encourages, supports, facilitates and develops these qualities in its people can be called a *learning organization* or a *learning company.* A learning organization is a group of people who learn not only as individuals but as a team. The process starts with a personal commitment. This is where character has a significant impact on the ability to execute a self-development process.

CHARACTER AND SELF-DISCIPLINE

The bedrock of character is self-discipline. Character and self-discipline are at the heart of being able to motivate and guide yourself, whether the objective is exercising, finishing a job or just getting up in the morning. Self-development depends on taking responsibility for learning. Personal improvement creates real benefits, including career development, improved job performance, satisfaction, contribution, developing specific skills and abilities and achieving one's potential, whether personally or professionally. The upside seems pretty convincing.

———— ◇ ————

The bedrock of character is self-discipline.

———— ◇ ————

PERSONAL MASTERY

"Personal mastery" is the term that Peter Senge (*The Fifth Discipline*) uses to describe a level of commitment that begins with competence and skill, and continues to develop from there. He uses the term to describe a process in which an individual approaches life as a creative work; or living life through personal design rather than reactive happenstance. He contends that organizations learn only through individuals who learn. Just because individuals are engaged in a personal learning process, however, does not guarantee organizational learning. But without individual learning, learning at the organizational level cannot occur.

——— ◇ ———

Self-development or self-mastery is at the heart of a successful learning organization.

——— ◇ ———

Learning, then, is not confined only to the acquisition of more knowledge or information. It also means to enhance your ability to produce results that you truly want to experience in life. Senge calls it "lifelong generative learning." A learning organization is not possible unless there are people throughout the organization who practice continuous learning from this perspective. The term *mastery* in itself may suggest dominance over people or things. But mastery also can mean a practiced level of proficiency, such as that of a master craftsperson or carpenter. Such a person does not dominate but, rather, leads from personal proficiency. People with a high level of personal mastery are in a continual learning mode. *They really never arrive—the journey is the reward.*

Self-development or self-mastery is at the heart of a successful learning organization. In part, the goal is not simply to gain knowledge, but also to learn how to use it. Guiding this process is a mentoring opportunity for management.

FOSTERING A CULTURE OF PERSONAL GROWTH AND MASTERY

PERSONAL CHOICE

Deciding to become involved in a program of personal growth is a matter of personal choice and commitment. Organizations cannot force their employees to participate in a personal mastery program. In fact, I recall a colleague whom I mentored several years ago when he was having particular difficulty with self-discipline. He was a young manager I had brought into the company. I really wanted to see him master not only the ability to manage himself, but to gain proficiency in all areas of management. He was very bright and truly hard-working. At the time, I was heavily influenced by material I had been studying on self-mastery and I was perhaps over-zealous in trying to get his enthusiasm to match mine. I fear that at times my mentoring was off-putting to him. I'm sure I failed to achieve the results I otherwise might have, had I taken a slightly more objective approach. Realizing that my mistake was part of my own learning process, my dear friend, attorney and life mentor, Roger Lageschulte, counseled me, "There's only a one-syllable difference between *mentor* and *tormentor!*"

As senior managers, a lot of us undoubtedly have gone through such experiences with the very best of intentions, yet have not achieved the results we hoped for. Although I learned a lot from my experience, I probably dampened my colleague's spirit for a while in terms of his commitment to self-mastery or self-development. Thank goodness he continued his career in a most effective way and, in fact, became very successful.

---- ◇ ----

There's only a one-syllable difference between
mentor and tormentor!

---- ◇ ----

Frequently, managers become zealots on behalf of whatever has worked for themselves. And that's something we want to be careful about as we attempt to develop a mentoring culture in which self-development and self-mastery are encouraged. It's all good stuff, but managers who have achieved a high level of proficiency, self-discipline and development should model their successes, rather than coercively impose their enthusiasm upon their colleagues. Mentors can encourage, facilitate and suggest. In the final analysis, however, mentees themselves must be motivated and committed to taking the steps necessary to achieve their own objectives.

MODELING

Part of the process of facilitating a mentoring program for continuous learning is to teach others about the process. First, participants need to understand the benefits to be gained so they have reason to become enthusiastic. There is much that can be done within the business culture to facilitate and encourage the process.

And that is the purpose of this book: to encourage, guide and facilitate readiness for the profound process of mentoring. That's really the only effective way management can be involved in self-development. The core leadership strategy is rather straightforward. Management needs to be the model.

———— ◇ ————

**Management's commitment to its own
personal mastery will attract others to the
process when they see the results.**

———— ◇ ————

Talking about personal mastery and introducing advantages and benefits may open minds, but seeing personal mastery in action will be the most convincing process. To sell it you have to live it.

A CYBERNETIC MODEL

The need to monitor a new system, particularly one so comprehensive as company-wide mentoring, cannot be overemphasized. The overall process resembles a cybernetic model. In "systems" jargon, a cybernetic model is one that is patterned on the thermostatic control principle. Constant temperature feedback (evaluation) produces adjustments to the heating/cooling mechanism (performance), which then produces a comfortable room temperature (results). In the context of the mentoring process, this analogy describes management's need for consistent feedback (evaluation) to determine whether the mentoring and learning activities (performance) are achieving the desired end (exceptional results).

In addition to ongoing evaluation of the components of the strategic process, I recommend at least biannual sessions in which senior management takes a comprehensive look at the system to see how it is doing. A good approach is to get feedback from all management and other participants. The human resources manager can provide periodic evaluations, after which senior management evaluates the results and makes adjustments as needed.

By now, you probably realize that this is a long-term strategy. Yet, there are early benefits. Like a very good wine, the results improve over time.

Mentor's Checkup

◇ Is your company preparing for the future? What strategy is in place to increase the likelihood of a bright outcome?

◇ Are business fundamentals an important part of your core training activities?

◇ What is the development climate in your organization? Is senior management openly supportive of personal growth?

PART II

WHOM TO MENTOR

CHAPTERS 6-8

CHAPTER SIX

MENTORING THE INDIVIDUAL

OVERVIEW

This chapter focuses on the basic building block of mentoring—the individual. It is the individual who determines to what extent growth and development will occur in an organization. If there is a keen desire by the individual to develop his or her career and a willingness to accept responsibility for that development, then the journey has begun. The first phase involves communicating an understanding and appreciation for self-development, self-mastery and proficiency.

———— ◇ ————

Ultimately, we are all judged by our results.

———— ◇ ————

Personal growth is aimed at improved performance. The goal of management in supporting a mentoring program is to encourage growth that can produce exceptional performance. It is hoped that the person being mentored also will receive the benefit of a more enriched career. Assessing one's abilities and determining areas for growth is a critical step in starting the development process. Optimally, this is initiated through self-assessment. Assessment aids are available to facilitate the evaluation process so you can create specific growth targets. These are briefly reviewed in this chapter.

THE STARTING POINT

Every process has a starting point. For mentoring, it begins with the individual, who needs to have a clear understanding of what the process entails and who is responsible for it. Otherwise, wasted time and disappointing results will follow. The old truism, "clarity is power," has great application throughout the mentoring process. Clarity regarding one's personal responsibility, strengths and weaknesses, and developmental goals greatly increases the likelihood of a successful mentoring experience.

PERSONAL RESPONSIBILITY

Taking responsibility for personal growth is the individual's first step toward that growth. The process cannot begin until this understanding is internalized. The only way we learn and develop is by personally guiding and facilitating the process. Attending classes, watching videos, reading relevant material, even experiencing one-on-one coaching can be just a lot of activity that doesn't necessarily produce the desired results. Until and unless a decision to acquire knowledge is made by each individual, the process will be disappointing. Learning occurs in relation to the degree that we personally lead, facilitate and manage our own learning. And what determines the level of effectiveness is attitude and personal awareness.

How one views the world—a person's paradigms—determines attitude. A positive attitude about learning, growing, developing and expanding knowledge is the fuel for a successful experience. For these reasons, an "attitude clarity check" at the outset is in order. Attitude determines how a person reacts to or feels about life experiences and views the world, which is manifested in one's behavior. Behavior produces results—both good and bad.

Behavior that is rewarded is repeated, especially if it elicits positive feelings. This principle is most obvious in the training of a child, although feeling appreciated and important are among the most basic and universal of human needs. This principle of behavior reinforcement is a wonderful little phenomenon that just keeps working for us all our lives. Those feelings of gratification are often experienced as competence, self-control or sense of purpose. These are the feelings that tend to support the learning process. And attitude is the driver.

Helping workers develop a positive, supportive attitude about self-development begins with a realistic look at reward and reinforcement mechanisms. The old "What's in it for me?" mechanism works pretty effectively most of our lives. If the "What's in it for me?" answer is positive and attractive, then a positive behavioral response usually follows. That's a pretty important threshold to cross. Each individual has to come to grips with the conclusion that, indeed, "There *is* something in it for me" in order to commit. Motivating participants to want to make that commitment represents an opportunity for senior management to create a powerful force within the organization.

And what an opportunity it is! Here's a chance to create one of the biggest win/win scenarios I have ever seen or experienced in corporate life. The future success of the business depends on capable people who remain in an ongoing developmental mode. Jobs will need to be filled by capable, knowledgeable workers. There are opportunities for people who have prepared themselves by acquiring the necessary knowledge and abilities. Does your company support and facilitate processes for individual growth and development on a company-wide basis? Getting people excited about their futures, committed to growth and development, creates a positive direction for a successful future for individuals and the business alike. It is a convergence of mutual need and benefit in which everybody wins.

——— ◇ ———

The future success of the business depends on capable people who remain in an ongoing developmental mode.

——— ◇ ———

There are organizations out there that have facilitated the development of a cadre of empowered workers. One can read about them in Tom Peters' books, Inc. Magazine, The Wall Street Journal, The Harvard Business Review, as well as other sources.

PERFORMANCE IS THE ISSUE

Performance and results. Performance and results. An endless cycle. And it follows that the better the performance, the better the results. Particularly for those who have capitalized on better performance. Capitalized. A good use of the word. It means to turn to advantage or profit. Turning processes to advantage is the result of strategic thinking. It reflects that an evaluative process occurred after which a preferred outcome was selected. And that's what management gets paid to do. Capitalizing on opportunities is the stuff of which successful companies and manager-leaders are made. They make choices that enhance the performance of the enterprise. Performance is the issue because we are measured by our results, individually and corporately.

INDIVIDUAL MENTORING STRATEGIES

Learning	Leading	Relating
Facilitate continuous individual learning	Facilitate individual leadership development	Facilitate developing individual relationship-building skills
As the basic building block of performance, Individual Learning involves a commitment to self-mastery and a continuous quest for knowledge. As conducting a successful business becomes increasingly knowledge-based (knowledge is power), the importance of individual learning is paramount.	Leadership occurs when individuals identify an opportunity to make something positive happen, and then take responsibility for the results. Followership, the essential companion, occurs when the leader offers a trustworthy direction. The best strategy creating followership is to provide a model others will follow.	People create results, and people working together accomplish even better results. Business usually requires people to work together for results. Therefore, effective people skills are an essential element of today's top business performers.

TABLE 6-1

Let's start with the end in mind and work back to square one. We want exceptional performance, individually and corporately. We won't get it corporately if we don't get it individually. To get exceptional individual performance as it is presented in our Strategic Mentoring Model (SMM) in Chapter Four, requires prowess in learning, leading and relating. These specific strategies, applied to the individual, are shown in Table 6-1. This is where we start the individual development process. It begins with an individual assessment, one that discloses the direction that development activities need to take.

This is the basic building block of the SMM— developing an individual development plan, addressing growth in knowledge, leadership and relationship-building skills. The individual development plan should include the following components:

◇   Individual assessment of skills and abilities

◇   Corporate opportunities and needs

◇   Career objectives

◇   Individual growth potential

◇   Specific growth targets

Each of these components will be described below to assist in developing a clear understanding of what is involved in constructing a meaningful development plan.

THE ASSESSMENT PROCESS

CHARACTERISTICS OF AN ACHIEVER

Many executives count their blessings when they discover they have a manager on their team who is at the top end of the performance scale. In the mentoring process, you need to identify these people early in their careers and continue to guide their development to help them remain at the upper end of the performance scale. For those aspiring to become proficient manager-leaders, it is important to identify the characteristics inherent in these high performers. I have described some of the characteristics of these promising, potentially excellent manager-leaders, in Table 6-2 below. They were then evaluated with the view that somehow they may fit into the Strategic Mentoring Model. This is what I observed:

The interrelationships among the nine strategies in the SMM also apply in terms of the individual achievement characteristics we wish to target in the mentoring process. Following is a brief discussion of each of the characteristics shown in the following grid (Table 6-2).

ACHIEVEMENT CHARACTERISTICS

	Learning	Leading	Relating
Individual	Thirst for knowledge	Takes responsibility	Character
Group/team	Shares knowledge	Encourager	Empathetic
Org./culture	Open to new ideas	Ambitiously forward looking	Image and reputation

TABLE 6-2

◊ *Thirst for Knowledge*–There is an attitude of wanting to develop skills and prepare to do the necessary work to succeed. The individual gladly accepts suggestions regarding articles or books to read or classes to take. Enthusiastically desires new information and is disciplined enough to manage self-directed learning.

◊ *Shares Knowledge*–Realizing knowledge drives the results, shares this knowledge with colleagues when given the opportunity to assist others in the learning process. Very good at spotting knowledge gaps and effectively contributing to bettering the situation.

◊ *Open to New Ideas*–This attitude really reflects the type of thinking that supports "the job is never done" or "good enough just isn't." Consistently wants to make something better; will not just accept the status quo but, instead, evaluates it to see what improvements can be made, looking for better ideas to improve results.

◊ *Takes Responsibility*–One of the most admirable features I've found in manager-leaders, whom I call "winners," is that they see voids and fill them. They continually look for opportunities to take responsibility to see that things get done. If no one is looking after a particular area of need, willingly steps up to it and sees that the job gets done—and done right.

◇ *Tenacious Encourager*—People face potentially upsetting situations almost daily. The ability to deal with the unexpected or the unpleasant requires a strength of focus and character. When emotions potentially can overwhelm concentration, then one easily can be diverted from what is truly important. Enthusiasm and persistence in the face of setbacks bode well for strong leadership and management success.

◇ *Ambitiously Forward-Looking*—High interest in career development and professional growth as a manager-leader. Motivated to develop their skill levels to enable participation at the highest-possible level in the management profession. Anticipation is the operative word here. Anticipate what is needed to get the preferred results. Forward-looking and thinks about the necessary steps to create what they want. Not only anticipate what they need to do, but also look out for their colleagues as well.

◇ *Character*—Character is the epicenter of values that drive behavior and support the development of followership. People will follow leaders with character whom they know they can depend on and who have values in which they can place confidence. Strong character, with a balanced value system, supports the development of followership. Strength of character, perhaps more than anything else, is identified by conviction to a set of values that produces ethical and predictable behavior.

◇ *Empathetic*—Leader-managers usually have specific expectations of the people they direct in terms of their work effort and accomplishments. If expectations are unreasonable, there is significant risk of followership suffering. Empathy is necessary if managers want to have successful subordinates who support their efforts. This goes beyond how much work effort is expected by the leader-manager. Even in day-to-day relationships, developing an understanding of the subordinate's problems, constraints and issues—being empathetic—will support a more effective management style.

◇ *Image and Reputation*—As irrational as it may seem, people do judge a book by its cover. Also, people react in a generally predictable manner to certain exterior qualities or the image that is presented. And this reaction varies significantly among industry sectors. Most people are generally more comfortable dealing with an element of predictability—and the "right" image supports predictability. Those managers who look and act like executives have a decided edge over those managers who do not convey the executive "image." On the surface, this may seem irrational, but managers who look after their image and reputation tend to be more successful than those who do not. At the heart of the issue is awareness and concern that implicitly or explicitly raises the question: "How effectively do I come across to those who look to me for leadership?" Of course, examples can be cited of leaders who succeeded in spite of image, however, such leaders are in the minority. Our objective is to provide guidelines that work for most of us. The total image you project, including your reputation, consists of many things. As noted, among the most important is the first impression you make on others; after that, factors that count include the depth and breadth of your knowledge, your flexibility, enthusiasm, character and sincerity. Qualities of which leaders are made.

——— ◇ ———

Character is the epicenter of values that drive behavior and support the development of followership.

——— ◇ ———

These characteristics describe potential manager-leaders who can make an incredible difference in business results. When such an individual is discovered, it represents an opportunity to organize as much work around them as is reasonable and, at the same time, to mentor them so they are taking on the necessary skills and abilities with which to handle even more responsibility. A serious investment opportunity has been identified.

Accordingly, individuals manifesting these characteristics are capable of stimulating other people in the organization to become high performers. Obviously, people of this sort are in high demand. Since there just aren't enough of them to go around, more need to be developed.

SELF-ASSESSMENT

In order to develop the rest of the organization, we need to begin with a self-assessment. The self-assessment exercises I have reviewed or used have covered the range, from pretty complicated to fairly straightforward. I prefer the latter. Whatever course is followed (although I urge the simplified version to begin with) it needs to be based on a rational model. Each assessment process utilizes the process of comparison. Some particular aspect of performance is compared to a standard or a goal. Since the goals are the basis for comparison, it is essential that we have a clear understanding of them in order to bring rationality to the process. Questions that contribute to clarity include:

◇ What values contribute to the development of these goals?

◇ Whose goals are these and why?

◇ Can I effectively adopt these goals as my own? Would I want to change them in some way?

Because we are considering self-assessment that will lead to self-development, the best approach is to use an individually led model.

Ultimately, the development process should result in some form of behavioral change. Your goal is improved personal performance. Performance emanates from behavior. Thus, improved performance results from modifying the previous behavior with a specific development or modification process, creating the new result.

This raises the questions, "*What* behavior do I change and how do I change it?" And most important, "*Why* do I change it?" These questions can be answered more effectively when considered in the full context of the results that are sought. The Development Process Model (Table 6-3) identifies the various steps involved in creating results. The process starts with the identification of needs to be satisfied.

DEVELOPMENT PROCESS MODEL

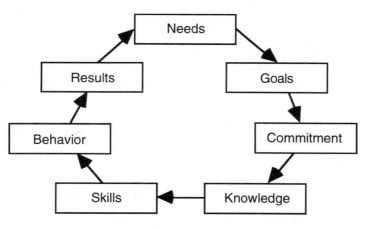

TABLE 6-3

The first step in the above assessment process is to determine whether the current results are meeting your needs. As an example, here is a personal growth situation that occurred while I was using the Development Process Model. Early in my career I was called upon to speak before fairly sizable audiences. This was very difficult for me. I lacked both experience and confidence. My *need* was to be able to speak comfortably and effectively before medium-to-large sized groups. Thus my *goal* was to develop my ability to do just that—become a competent public speaker. There were several options open to me. A speakers' bureau was accessible and no doubt would have been a good choice. But the more challenging and interesting option was to teach a class in supervision at an inner-city community college. (Maybe my students should have been asked if they wanted to participate in my personal development.)

In any event, I realized that if this were to be a successful experience for my students and myself, I was going to have to become a very good instructor. And that became my *commitment*—to be the best instructor these students had ever had. I worked hard to achieve my goal. I prepared. Then I prepared some more. When I stood up in front of the class, I had the confidence of really knowing my material; thus part of the *knowledge* from the model was satisfied. The next step was to determine what I could do to make it interesting and invigorating for them. I analyzed the delivery techniques of speakers I particularly admired. I identified their *skills* and determined to make them my own. I read about public speaking. I discussed public speaking with successful speakers. Then I set out to create successful "performances" based on my knowledge of the skills I needed to develop. My speaking *behavior* occurred one night a week for three hours. So my task was to speak for three hours, hopefully disseminating absolutely riveting information that would have my students sitting on the edges of their chairs.

Successful speakers learn to read their audiences to get immediate feedback. As a speaker, there are lots of good measures of whether you are retaining interest, including eye contact, restlessness, yawning, drooping eyelids, nodding off, and the like. To avoid this kind of response requires variation in delivery, while providing meaningful information. To make sure I was on the right track, I developed an "instructor assessment" form that included essential items such as content, application, and quality of presentation. Also, open-ended "I would like more..." and "I could do with less..." opportunities were included. I used the form about every four weeks during my first year of teaching and every couple of months in the subsequent three years that I continued to teach. I am indebted to a number of very conscientious students for their feedback in guiding my development. My *behavior*, my instructing performance, created the desired results. I developed a speaking ability that enabled me, with confidence, to address most any group comfortably. During my development process, I continually compared my results with my needs. The process continued while I worked on knowledge, skills and behavior until the results satisfied the need. Now I use this model extensively in my mentoring.

CORPORATE OPPORTUNITIES AND NEEDS

In the above development example, one thing was missing. The organization I was working for didn't help me accelerate the process; nor did they identify at an early point the opportunity that would have allowed me to get started sooner. My management knew my success would be enhanced, and so would theirs, if this particular skill, along with several others, were facilitated sooner rather than later. My very real contribution to the results of the enterprise could have been increased sooner. I was motivated. My management did do a very effective job of selecting career-oriented individuals who were motivated to develop their abilities. But there wasn't a program in place to support these kinds of personal efforts. I don't think that management ever considered what could be achieved. Their support came at a much broader level.

Individually, I assessed the need and the opportunity for my development. The point here is that if this had been incorporated into the company's overall development strategy, facilitated by management in some form, earlier benefits could have been realized by myself and by the organization. The opportunity for the organization is to identify corporate needs for exceptional performance, the corollary skill requirements, and then facilitate development. In addition, there are fundamental business skills, described in the above example, that need to be assessed; also development opportunities need to be facilitated. This is an opportunity that is increasing in frequency and need as business becomes more reliant on the knowledge worker. A comprehensive development strategy, based on individual assessments, can provide one of the most meaningful investment opportunities for a successful business future.

CAREER OBJECTIVE

Individually, continuous learning and development will be most effective when aligned with career objectives. Random learning may be worthwhile, but it is not as effective as it is when targeted at a specific goal, such as furthering one's career. Goal-oriented learning requires a fairly clear understanding of career direction, opportunities and development needs.

I have seen many judgment errors made (and I have made my share) in promoting individuals into positions for which they were not quite ready. This is one of the most pervasive problems in business management. Companies are still promoting the best salespeople, computer specialists, engineers, accountants, and marketing specialists into management positions without providing adequate training and development. A lot of them make the transition. But quite a few don't, and then the result usually is the loss of a good pre-management contributor and an underperforming department. This is very expensive turnover. We not only lose the good worker but the momentum during the unsuccessful management transition. While this is difficult to measure, it nevertheless is significant.

——— ◇ ———

Continuous learning and development will be most effective when aligned with career objectives. Random learning may be worthwhile, but it is not as effective as it is when targeted at a specific goal.

——— ◇ ———

A careful screening for realistic career objectives, supported by management-facilitated development, can be a proactive solution to future management needs. Companies that enjoy prolonged business success have as one of their major contributors a joint career development program with their employees. A strategic mentoring program can be such a catalyst.

INDIVIDUAL GROWTH POTENTIAL

One of the more discouraging results is to be facilitating the growth of someone who is bumping against his developmental "ceiling" or limit. Very important to the assessment process is the consideration of growth potential. And I urge extreme caution. This is not a precise process in most cases. Essentially, it's a position or state with which the particular individual must come to grips. This can be based on a comprehensive evaluation process. Also, this can most effectively be accomplished in a mentoring context. I want to stress the importance of the individual becoming aware of this potential problem. The evaluation process represents a concern that one not overreach his capabilities. A stretch can be beneficial. But to take on responsibility that demands significantly more than an individual has to offer can be dangerous. It can also be a very seductive process, particularly when one is motivated to advance one's career.

———— ◇ ————

**Knowing your weaknesses and limitations
can be more important than knowing
only your areas of prowess.**

———— ◇ ————

You can get into more trouble by not knowing your limitations than by knowing only your strengths. Clarity regarding one's limitations enables a positive response. Then you can factor in your compensating strategy. Developing an understanding of limitations is a focused exercise that should take place at the outset of any development process.

There are two methods I recommend as the starting point for self-assessment and evaluation of growth potential. Both ultimately result in a review and discussion with a mentor.

SPECIFIC GROWTH TARGETS

A comprehensive plan with specific growth targets will assist in realizing the greatest growth benefit for both the individual and the organization. Both individuals and businesses need to develop in ways that will support the realization of long-term success. Management benefits by recognizing the common goal, and by supporting it. The individual benefits by increasing his abilities and value to the business.

A comprehensive human-resource-development plan is an important piece of work to guide this strategic process. Regrettably, not very many of these development plans are produced and implemented so that they capitalize on the enormously positive results such plans can produce.

This is one huge opportunity for any business, but particularly the small-to-medium-sized business emerging from entrepreneurial leadership. One problem often encountered in this particular business segment is the lack of a professional or practiced human-resource staff who has the capability to develop such a plan. One can make a strong case for engaging professional assistance to develop the staff so it is able to produce and manage this process on an ongoing basis.

—— ◇ ——

The comprehensive human-resource development plan
provides the essential direction for development.
Mentoring is the most effective facilitating
force to bring it to reality.

—— ◇ ——

THE MENTORING PROCESS

Much has now been presented about the benefits of a comprehensive mentoring strategy to facilitate human resource development. Until one has seen, or better yet, experienced the process, description hardly does it justice. Mentoring can occur at all levels in an organization and in varying forms. The basic process occurs between the mentor and mentee, one-on-one, as described in Chapter One. Although there are numerous permutations, the essential operating unit is the individual. (The roles of the mentor and mentee are developed in Chapters Twelve and Thirteen).

One of the best examples of mentoring in action is found in a fast-paced, management-adventure novel, *The Goal*, by Eli Goldratt. The concept of mentoring is introduced in a subtle interaction between the leading character, Alex Rogo, a harried plant manager, and an old college chum, Jonah, from whom he is seeking counsel. Through a chance meeting with Jonah, Alex Rogo begins to describe the serious problems he is experiencing at the plant he manages. In fact, his plant's overall performance is in such a dire state that he has just been informed he has only ninety days in which to turn it around or corporate headquarters will close it.

What follows is a series of just-in-the-nick-of-time meetings that save the company. In these meetings, Jonah helps Alex break out of his conventional thinking to see what needs to be done before it's too late. The reader "sits in" on these "mentoring" sessions to see how Jonah guides Rogo through the analytical processes necessary to develop his own solutions. The author has described what happens in the story: "Jonah, despite his knowledge of the solutions, provokes Alex to arrive at his own answers by supplying question marks rather than exclamation marks."

While the story itself is engaging, it also provides a working model of the mentoring process. I highly recommend this book as a step toward expanding your awareness and appreciation of mentoring dynamics. A few years ago I used this book in a book discussion group with about fourteen of my managers. The company had three divisions: manufacturing, wholesale, and retail. Managers attended from all three divisions. In addition to gaining a greater appreciation for mentoring, several significant opportunities for improved inter-divisional efficiencies emerged. A CEO's dream come true!

Management's goal in a comprehensive mentoring process is to foster an environment that encourages continual development. In order for this to happen, the senior management team is the best model. Each manager on the senior management team needs to understand how to be a Jonah in facilitating, guiding and encouraging individuals toward excellence. Everyone in the organization relies on senior management to get it right—a huge responsibility!

MENTOR'S CHECKUP

◇ How would you describe your commitment to personal growth? How would others describe your commitment and your competence?

◇ How can you envision the Strategic Mentoring Model affecting your organization?

◇ How would you evaluate yourself in terms of the characteristics of an achiever identified in Table 6-1?

◇ What are your personal-growth targets? How do you plan to achieve them?

CHAPTER SEVEN

MENTORING THE GROUP/TEAM

OVERVIEW

The first part of this chapter is devoted to the evolution of groups into teams. The progression includes consideration of group forms, effectiveness criteria, and then the metamorphosis from group to team, with particular emphasis on empowerment and emotional intelligence.

Work teams are becoming the work unit in the marketplace, especially in knowledge-oriented businesses. As a result, those with the necessary social skills to make teams more effective increasingly are in demand. The changing role from individual to group member creates new needs and opportunities for human-resource development. Yet, preparing individuals to adapt to the new demands of group-oriented work supports greater productivity. The most effective strategy for achieving this transition is comprehensive group mentoring.

Group or team mentoring starts with consideration of the behaviors that produce performance excellence. The Strategic Mentoring Model, as discussed in Chapter Five, identifies three group/team-excellence strategies—learning, leading and relating. The chapter concludes with descriptions of real situations encountered in the implementation and development of teams by the writer.

——— ◊ ———

**Work teams are becoming
the work unit in the marketplace.**

——— ◊ ———

The only reason groups should be formed is so that members can learn from each other, and learn together, in order to accomplish individual, team and organizational goals. Mentoring the process significantly increases the likelihood of achieving the desired goals.

WHAT IS A GROUP?

Increasingly, work is being accomplished in small workplace groups. Organization and management specialists, such as Peter Drucker, anticipate that by the end of this decade one-third of the American workforce will be comprised largely of *knowledge workers.* This new identity is given to people whose productivity is based on adding value to information. Drucker, who coined the term "knowledge worker," also points out that such workers' expertise is usually quite specialized. And, significantly, *their productivity depends on the coordination of their efforts as part of an organizational team.* The work group is the work unit of the future.

Such a group is differentiated from the team; the major difference has to do with effectiveness. My definition of a team is a group that has achieved a state of effectiveness as a cohesive, productive unit. In this state, a team is capable of outperforming a group comprised of similar individuals who are functioning solitarily. Before we explore the differences further, let's take a close look at the characteristics of a group.

GROUP CHARACTERISTICS

◇ *Membership*–Two or more people interacting for more than a few minutes.

◇ *Needs*–Members form a group to satisfy common needs.

◇ *Goals*–Members hold common aims or goals that, to some extent, bind them together.

◇ *Perception*–Members are collectively conscious of their membership in a group.

◇ *Interdependence*–Members are affected by and respond to events that affect any other members of the group.

◇ *Interaction*–Members influence and respond to one another in the process of communicating.

◇ *Cohesiveness*–Members want to be in the group and join in its activities to contribute to the group purpose.

◇ *Social organization*–A group may be seen as a specific and unified social or work unit with social norms and relationships.

Each of the identified characteristics represents an important aspect but none by itself defines a group. Also, not all of the characteristics are expected to apply to every group. These characteristics are offered primarily to raise our level of understanding about groups. In the organizational context, groups represent a resource. Optimizing, or making the group's performance more effective will lead us to a discussion about the distinctives of a team. But first, let's consider group size and related implications on work.

GROUP SIZE

Group size affects the social dynamics of the group, which in turn affects the relative ease or difficulty of guiding the group performance. Below is a comparison of group size and changing characteristics.

CHANGING CHARACTERISTICS OF GROUPS

# of Members	Changing Characteristics
2-6	Little structure or organization required; leadership fluid.
7-12	Structure and differentiation of roles begins. Face-to-face interaction less frequent.
12-25	Structure and role differentiation critical. Sub-groups emerge. Face-to-face interaction difficult.
>25	Positive leadership critical to success. Greater anonymity; sub-groups form. Communication more complex.

TABLE 7-1

As the size of the group increases, skills that are needed to provide leadership change. In addition, relationships become more complex, requiring higher-level skills to manage and/or lead. What happens in most organizations is that the group size increases to meet new work demands, but the strengthening of leadership and management skills usually lags seriously, if it is addressed at all. Thus, the efficiency of these important resources very often remains underdeveloped.

TYPICAL GROUP FORMS

One of the first principles that managers learn about organization and management is "form follows function." The application of this principle creates groups, as does the creation of classes of workers, such as "middle management" or "supervisors." Following is a partial list of groups that develop as the organization grows.

TYPICAL WORK GROUPS

- ◇ Senior management
- ◇ Project team
- ◇ Task force
- ◇ Committee
- ◇ Middle management
- ◇ Service group
- ◇ Secretarial group

- ◇ Supervisors
- ◇ Departments
- ◇ Divisions
- ◇ Product group
- ◇ Executive staff
- ◇ Boards of directors
- ◇ Sales teams

Each work group has its own set of operating criteria, purposes, and objectives. Each usually has some form of leadership and/or management. As organizations grow, management often overlooks the extent to which work group members can develop to become more effective contributors. As the potential impact of these various groups is considered, one can quickly see the potential benefit of fielding the best-prepared players rather than an underprepared group.

———— ◇ ————

In the sports world, championship games are won by championship players. Championship players are the result of a concentrated development plan.

———— ◇ ————

We can learn championship lessons from our sports colleagues. Preparation is everything.

GROUP EFFECTIVENESS CRITERIA

To assure that a group has a good shot at being effective, three aspects should be considered. I call these the three C's of effectiveness: clarity, composition and conventions. The manager-leader responsible for the group performance would do well to assess the particular group's experience, training and proficiency in order to determine what aspects should be addressed to raise performance levels.

CLARITY

Making certain that the group understands its purpose and mission is the first task. Otherwise, the group resources are inadequately or wrongly focused. As a result, the group is unable to deliver its best effort. To really get the level of clarity necessary to support high performance, the following clarity-enhancing steps should be taken:

- ◇ Individual roles defined.
- ◇ Communication and feedback mechanisms established.
- ◇ Time constraints understood.
- ◇ Relationships with other groups understood.
- ◇ Performance expectations described.
- ◇ Resources defined.
- ◇ Support services identified.

COMPOSITION

To achieve the best results requires the best people. Properly staffing the group with the right "players," both in terms of numbers and abilities, is essential for top performance. The manager-leader is urged to spend quality time assessing the skill requirements and head count necessary to achieve the preferred results. Then, a careful selection of personnel should follow to match the skill requirements to the mission of the group.

CONVENTIONS

The conventions are the "rules of the game." These identify what is acceptable and what is not, normally expressed as "expectations." This gives the manager-leader the opportunity to confirm that group norms are clear in order to encourage optimum group behavior. One of my favorites here relates to meetings. My meetings start on time—with whoever has arrived at the prescribed starting time. Huge amounts of time get wasted as a result of sloppy meeting discipline. The leader-manager, that is, the group leader, is accountable for that time. Establishing realistic, sensible group conventions will increase the group's effectiveness.

METAMORPHOSIS—
FROM GROUP TO TEAM

So far in this chapter the material has focused on the group. The group processes and dynamics within the organization are important contributors to its success. The future of business will involve an ever-increasing phenomenon of clusters of knowledge workers.

Management's opportunity is to empower group members, thus creating teams. That is, the group in which the individuals are functioning should achieve an empowered state that takes advantage of the full talent of its members. This empowered group, which is capable of delivering exceptional results, is a team. But hold on. "Empowered" is such an overused term that the full meaning and significance of what a team really is may not be readily understood.

Not all groups are teams, just as not all individual performers are stars. A team is a group that has become a star. What we want to understand is how groups can become stars so we can then mentor our groups to stardom. The legendary manager of the New York Yankees baseball team, Casey Stengel, once commented that "It is not difficult to find stars. The difficulty is getting them to play together." And that is the difference between a group and a team. A team emerges when the stars play together.

—— ◇ ——

Management's opportunity is to empower group
members, thus creating teams.

—— ◇ ——

In Chapter One, performance that is specific to star players was identified. Where performance and results can be judged exceptional, I have found the following phenomena to be present:

◇ Knowledge

◇ Responsibility

◇ Harmony

◇ Self mastery

◇ Effective teams

◇ Empowering culture

These qualities have their origins in individual competence; that is, in learning, leading and relating. These three characteristics of exceptional performance are the foundation for the Strategic Mentoring Model introduced in Chapter Four. The same performance conclusions apply to the group. As individual members become highly competent practitioners in these three performance areas, the team develops and becomes capable of producing exceptional performance.

TEAM DISTINCTIVES

IMPORTANCE OF RELATIONSHIPS

As a result of having mentored individuals and teams over the years, certain performance distinctives have become evident. I have worked with some individuals who have become quite competent at learning, absolutely devouring information, impressively expanding their knowledge. I have also worked with others who have understood the nuances of leadership/followership and were quite skilled at building consensus. But it's the third characteristic of performance, relating, that is the most significant, particularly when it comes to team-building.

Teams and teamwork only exist to the extent effective relationships exist. Relationship is the artery that distributes the lifeblood among the vital organs, the individual team members. Poor relationships yield poor team performance. Great relationships support great team performance. I can't say categorically that only great relationships produce great results. But I will say great results are unlikely unless there are great relationships.

TEAM GROUND RULES

In my various corporate adventures, immediately upon assuming the CEO position, I make it a priority to meet with my direct subordinates, whom I refer to as the executive team. It is always helpful to let folks know early on what kind of corporate culture the new guy will want to see operating. I will save the full message on culture until the next chapter, but in relation to the team, my introductory remarks usually go something like this:

> As we begin to work together now to produce the very best business results we can, there needs to be clarity about our working relationships. It will be productive for all of us to be on the same wavelength regarding conventions of behavior. Central to the establishment of an effective executive team is to have relationships based on treating one another with dignity and respect. And we need to be the models for the whole organization.
>
> Next in importance is a sense of unity and harmony. I fully expect passion to be manifested when we believe a proposed course of action needs further consideration. In fact, it's essential. However, we need to conduct our business, and our relationships, on the basis that the best thinking will come from a team working in a harmonious way. Conflict is like throwing sand into the machinery of creativity. It just grinds effective operations and communication to a halt. Harsh words cripple creativity and diminish one's dignity. A unified team is capable of far better performance than one preoccupied with strife and conflict. Our battles will occur with water pistols, not swords. Passion with humor and goodwill is a most effective strategy for building collegial relationships.
>
> The better our relationships, the more effectively we can address business issues. Then relationship problems don't get

in the way. An important element of developing this condition is commitment to one another's success. If one team member hurts, we all hurt. Treat your colleague as your customer. If your customer has a problem, so do you. You should be aware of your colleagues' needs and concerns and, where possible, become (or at least help with) the solution.

Finally, a few words about communication. I need to know the important stuff and so do you. Not only that, we need to be assured that important information is getting where it needs to go, on a timely basis. That is a responsibility we all have. In order to facilitate that, I would like to meet with each of you weekly, one-on-one, as you prepare the agenda. The objective is to identify the matters that need addressing on a timely basis to keep the business moving ahead. We don't want to be the bottle-neck. We want to be the facilitators and the catalysts. Then, as a team, we will meet either every week or every other week, depending on need, to assess how we are doing. We all should be guided by the no-surprises philosophy, except on our birthdays.

---- ◇ ----

Central to the establishment of an effective executive team are relationships based on treating one another with dignity and respect. And we need to be the models for the whole organization.

---- ◇ ----

After that initial meeting, folks are pretty clear on my beliefs and expectations of business relations that support excellence. In the context of my talk, I emphasize the importance of dignity, respect, harmony, rapport, empathy, cooperation and communication in our relationships, all of which are essential for peak team performance.

I usually don't get into character issues such as honesty, trust and integrity. I will take it on faith that those are in place until shown otherwise. Besides, there are better forums in which to discuss character issues. Different people have different sensitivities to character-related discussions. I like to wait until I know my colleagues a bit better before discussing issues that some might consider more personal. However, during subsequent mentoring opportunities, the effective use of questions often can open doors to sensitive issues. The strategy of asking the right question at the right time is addressed in Chapter Twelve, "Deciding To Be A Mentor."

MENTORING THE TEAM

The groundwork now has been laid for a close look at what is involved in team mentoring. From the Strategic Mentoring Model in Figure 4-3 there are three strategies that pertain to the group/team.

TEAM MENTORING STRATEGIES

Learning	Leading	Relating
Facilitate continuous learning on building team excellence	Facilitate team leadership development	Facilitate developing team relationship building skills
The advantage of working groups is the collective knowledge and skills that may be used in achieving a goal. Especially effective is a group that also begins to learn together from sources within and outside the group.	Many successful businesses are led by small teams that may be found at any level within the management hierarchy. Increasing team leadership capabilities helps create even more internal resources that can be used towards achieving good business results.	Groups that work well together have greater opportunity for achieving good results. Group success depends on building member relationships and drawing upon the abilities of all members.

TABLE 7-2

To effectively implement these three strategies, the behaviors that should produce the desired results need to be identified. These behaviors become the mentoring focus. An evaluation of the highly successful teams I have worked with, as well as examination of the success of others, led to the development of the following team-mentoring objectives.

TEAM MENTORING OBJECTIVES

Learning	Leading	Relating
Team building	Building consensus	Harmonizing
Self-mastery	Developing followership	Create rapport
Emotional intelligence	Sharing initiative	Empathetic
Cooperative		
Trustworthy		
Communicator		

TABLE 7-3

These mentoring objectives are based on performance distinctives (Table 7-3), which are a combination of character attributes and people-handling skills. As a mentor, I generally focus on awareness-building regarding what creates good working relationships and what they contribute to the team effort.

——— ◇ ———

As knowledge-based work groups and intellectual capital become a more significant part of a business' human resource balance sheet, improving the way people work together will make a critical competitive difference.

——— ◇ ———

Each of these elements is a part of our "emotional intelligence," a concept introduced by psychologist Daniel Goleman in his book of the same title. His book quickly became a bestseller because, among other reasons, the author corroborated something that many of us had a hunch was true, but for which there had been no scientific evidence. The author explains that emotional intelligence, rather than "high-IQ" intelligence, makes a significant contribution to successful business performance. Goleman writes that emotional intelligence, which is integral to relationship skills, is not fixed at birth. In fact, he contends, emotional intelligence can be nurtured and strengthened throughout life. An apt goal for mentoring!

In fact, it is emotional intelligence that is the heart and soul of teamwork. It is the source of organizational savvy that enables individuals, working effectively together, to produce exceptional performances.

What follows is a brief description of each of the mentoring objectives, shown under the heading of one of the three team-mentoring strategies. The description is provided to assist in identifying the performance ability that is sought.

Learning—The place to start building team prowess is in the area of knowledge and awareness. Knowing the specific performance behaviors that contribute to exceptional team performance is the essential starting point. In the workplace, knowledge is power. And this is powerful knowledge.

—— ◇ ——

Emotional intelligence is the source of organizational savvy that enables individuals, working effectively together, to produce exceptional performances.

—— ◇ ——

Team Building—Developing an understanding of teams is the first building block. This process should include information on how teams function, processes to encourage participation, what makes them work, and how to develop them. An understanding of where to begin should emerge.

Self-Mastery—Self-mastery as a team member addresses the need for personal discipline in order to carry out the role identified above. The process begins with acquisition of knowledge and the ability to perform in a team setting. Essentially, it's the disciplined application of all that is learned and developed in the team-mentoring program.

Emotional Intelligence—Developing an understanding of what constitutes emotional intelligence can be an integral part of nurturing and developing one's team-based skills. Developing insights into work cells and what behavioral strategies are most effective to accomplish quality results is what manager-leaders need to know to be effective in their jobs.

———— ◇ ————

**The dynamics of the team create multiple leaders.
Thus, leadership and followership are
fluctuating responsibilities.**

———— ◇ ————

Leading—Team leadership requires a delicate balance between leading and following. The size of the team will impact the particular leadership style and needs. The leadership role often becomes that of a leader-among-equals. Then, each member willingly provides follower-ship as leadership is needed. A wonderful description of this type of leadership appeared in a book titled *Servant Leadership* by Robert Greenleaf. Servant-leadership occurs when the leader is first servant. Greenleaf writes that natural feelings make one want to serve; that is, to serve first. Then conscious choice, based on meeting a need, creates a desire to lead. That is precisely the kind of leadership required to bring teams to excellence. And this kind of leadership is particularly appropriate for teams of knowledge workers. Following are the performance objectives of team leaders.

Building Consensus—One of the processes in the team environment that elicits creative participation is con-sensus-building. Assuring that differing views get aired and considered is an important responsibility of the leader. Facilitating competing ideas in a harmonious setting requires knowledge of technique and skill. In order to achieve consensus, each member must listen and develop an understanding. The leader will place emphasis on the former to achieve the latter.

Building Followership—The corollary to good leadership is solid followership. The dynamics of the team create multiple leaders. Thus, leadership and followership are fluctuating responsibilities. Awareness and perception are good catalysts to develop a sense of when to lead and when to follow.

Sharing Initiative—All team members should come to the task prepared to both assume and share initiative. With multiple leaders, participants should be prepared to share responsibility for initiatives and results. Empathy and perspective are valuable aids in facilitating the way that each member views the team's needs, processes and goals.

Relationship Skills—Successful leadership, team management and even team participation are inherent in the relationship skills. Not only are these important business skills, they are life skills. People who have mastered relationship-building skills have created a powerful resource for the future. At least 85 percent of senior managers' success is based on skills in this area.

———— ◇ ————

Having principles that consistently guide one's behavior create predictability, which leads to trust. Much of what builds positive relationship dynamics is based on trust.

———— ◇ ————

Harmonizing–Social harmony in a group, all things being equal, enables all members to contribute their talents and skills. Harmonizing provides the creative catalyst for participation, which is the first step toward contribution. This is the single most important element in producing effective working relationships.

Creates Rapport–Rapport is a close cousin to harmonizing. In fact, it is a significant contributor to and a preliminary step in the harmonizing process. Rapport signals a relationship marked by agreement, alignment or similarity. Rapport starts with the players becoming of "like mind" or getting on the same "wavelength"–meeting people on their own level.

Empathetic–The desire and ability to understand the other person's viewpoint is important in developing a positive relationship. Empathy communicates first that you care; second, you are interested; and third, you are open to another opinion rather than being close-minded. All three are essential to development of trust and respect.

Cooperative–A cooperative attitude indicates an openness to views and opinions other than your own–you don't have to have your way every time. Respect for others' thoughts and feelings is communicated. Participation is encouraged, which contributes to harmony.

Trustworthy–Consistency in behavior comes from character. Having principles that consistently guide one's behavior creates predictability, which leads to trust. Much of building positive relationship dynamics is based on trust.

Skilled Communicator–The ability to articulate the nuances around the direct message adds color, meaning and quality. More than half of communication is nonverbal. Alignment and attunement lend further refinement to the communication process. Mastering these elements provides significant skill in communicating meaning more fully, thus greatly enhancing performance.

TEAM COMPOSITION

TWO PHASES OF DEVELOPMENT

Ultimately, someone is responsible for a team's performance. As CEO, it has always been very clear that the executive team's performance was my responsibility. Being responsible for performance requires one to take action, provide support and encouragement, make team changes, and a whole lot more. For the next several pages, I will relate a few experiences and insights into mentoring an executive team.

———— ◇ ————

Nobody ever achieves perfect performance.
So we constantly deal with trade-offs.

———— ◇ ————

Most of the executive teams I have worked with have been inherited. As mentioned in an earlier chapter, my arrival at a new company has usually been prompted by change; the business needed transitioning to the next phase of development. My responsibilities have included getting the business to the desired performance levels. This would involve an evaluation of the management team as a start. The big question for each member of this team was this: "Can you contribute to this team what is needed to achieve the desired results?" Anyone who has managed a company through an executive team knows the answer to this question is not usually immediately forthcoming. Usually several months, preferably a business cycle, are necessary to assess the performance and contribution of a senior manager. Unless, of course, there are some obvious problems that quickly become identifiable.

There are at least two phases involved in the development of the executive team. There is an initial adjustment I usually make after assuming responsibility for the team. Then there is the longer-term development, working to improve the functioning of the team. The first phase—assessment and adjustment—essentially entails determining each person's level of development. This usually involves some skills assessment process, which then provides a guide for further development.

After that phase is completed, it then becomes crucial to facilitate the development of the individual skills of the executive staff so they can function as effectively as possible as an executive team. At this point, a mentoring program can begin.

DIVERSITY

The team is never perfect. There will always be a weak player. Nobody ever achieves perfect performance. So we constantly deal with trade-offs. The big question CEOs and senior managers constantly grapple with is this: Is the performance we are getting acceptable? I'm not suggesting that we start out by accepting less-than-sterling performances. However, there comes a point with each team member when you have to decide whether or not the performance he is delivering is acceptable. And it's usually a trade-off. My rule of thumb is that if the individual player is "above the 85 percent threshold of performance," in other words, he gets it right most of the time, then he should be on the team. I can work with him if he has the right attitude and is making a constructive contribution.

———— ◇ ————

Teams are a question of balance. What is needed
is not sameness but, rather, individuals who
balance well with one another.

———— ◇ ————

Sameness is not the objective either. But diversity needs to make sense. Team composition needs to be drawn from those who possess strengths or characteristics that meet a need and contribute to the overall strength. Teams are a question of balance. What is needed is not sameness but, rather, individuals who balance well with one another. In fact, diversity can be a plus, as long as it adds to the whole. In that way, one member's weakness can be offset by another's strength and their combined strengths used to full advantage.

CHAMPIONSHIP TEAMS

There are so many parallels between managing a business and managing a sports team. To achieve championship status as a sports team means fielding the best possible individual players who function exceedingly well as a team. Players are "changed" (a euphemism for fired or traded) until the team composition is determined to be capable of high-level performance. The same applies to business, although trading players usually is limited to internal maneuvers within the larger organizations. The point is that it is not fair to the individual players, the team, nor to the business to carry a player who lowers or negatively impacts the overall level of team play. Each player needs to contribute positively to the overall team process. If not, you can't afford to keep them.

Once the team is judged to be in place; that is, the players are in place who are top performers individually and can function well in the team mode, the stage is set for team mentoring. It's time to play ball.

TEAM MENTORING

Mentoring the team occurs at two levels. First, at an individual level. The specific strategies have been presented earlier that support mentoring individuals to achieve proficiency in functioning as a member of a team. The second level of mentoring is to the team. The starting point is with the Six Principles for Exceptional Performance (Table 4-1).

The objective of team mentoring is to get the team to perform together in a state that will create exceptional performance. This includes getting team member buy-in and support of what the team is trying to achieve. In this case, as both CEO and mentor, I want their support and commitment to manage the company, with their very significant involvement to create a culture that emphasizes individual excellence.

While individual development activities need to be focused on learning, leading and relating, the executive team needs to be focused on developing corporate performance. There are five priority areas on which to focus corporate performance. There are others, but to start with, these five are recommended to keep the effort focused.

◇   Performance management

◇   Financial management

◇   Business analyses

◇   Organizational development

◇   New business proposals

No priority is intended in the order. None should dominate to the extent it lessens the impact of any other. All five need to be central to the thinking and leadership of the executive team. Without a doubt a separate chapter, if not a book, could be devoted to each. The thrust of the presentation at this point is to emphasize the importance of the CEO actually mentoring development of the executive team in these five areas. A brief discussion of mentoring for performance in each of the five areas follows:

PERFORMANCE MANAGEMENT

The benefits of performance management are many. When you can't measure performance, managing it is quite difficult. Not impossible, but certainly communicating how you are managing performance is seriously handicapped. As a result, this is one of the first things you should examine. How is work managed? Within each department, measurement techniques will differ significantly. But you can expect each department head to develop a process that he can communicate to you that shows the work is being managed effectively. Performance ratios are valuable tools and facilitate communication and understanding regarding critical performance areas. Well-managed businesses track performance and react quickly to negative variations.

FINANCIAL MANAGEMENT

Financial planning and administration is the heart of a successful business. A strong chief financial officer and analytical support staff is a must. More businesses get into trouble because of lack of competent financial management than for any other reason. Financial management needs to occur not only in the finance department but in the financial units throughout the company. Today, all of management needs to understand and participate in the financial elements of running the company.

Monthly budget meetings offer an excellent opportunity to mentor the executive team in carrying the financial gospel throughout the business. The company's financial goals, strategies and performance need to be understood, supported and woven into the company's practices. This is not a problem in most publicly traded companies. However, in many mid-sized companies, the financial performance of the company is a mystery. To create an empowered performance-oriented management team, that must change.

———— ◇ ————

More businesses get into trouble because of lack of competent financial management than for any other reason.

———— ◇ ————

BUSINESS ANALYSES

A useful business tool that has become a valued companion of mine is the "SWOT" analysis (as discussed earlier)—evaluating the *strengths, weaknesses, opportunities* and *threats* of any particular proposal. This is a tool that not only should be used annually in looking at the budget strategies, but also should be used in looking at any new product proposal or when evaluating system changes. Having a manager or staff person go through this process and make a presentation to his colleagues creates a tremendous growth opportunity for everyone involved and a specific mentoring opportunity. Accomplishing this in a way that is a positive growing experience can be stimulating to emerging management talent.

Growth exercises of this type can be used to teach resourcefulness, the concept of completed staff work (that addresses all of the issues and provides reasoned options) and the development of a well-reasoned proposal. Not everyone knows how to go through these processes and somewhere it has to be taught, modeled, experienced and learned. I have been very surprised at the number of executives I've worked with who didn't know what a SWOT analysis is. Maybe they were doing similar activities under another name. However, having a clear strategy on which to evaluate business opportunities is a valuable tool for our management colleagues to use on a regular basis.

New Business Proposals

In some organizations, particularly smaller ones, the chief executive usually doesn't need to set up much of a process to review and evaluate new products or new system proposals. However, in the development of his or her managers, creating a forum for new ideas to be presented and challenged can be an exhilarating and positive developmental process.

In one business I managed, new product development was a crucial part of our enterprise. My group marketing director was responsible for introducing new product concepts and strategies. He had developed an excellent SWOT analysis-and-presentation format that facilitated a healthy evaluative forum. I am sure two or three of us could have met in my office and hashed out a preferred direction without the involvement of half-a-dozen department heads. Including them in the process, however, expanded the buy-in as well as the learning process of what we looked for in selecting strategic processes and products. It enabled the mentoring of this important method of evaluation and presentation, which has now been woven into the business culture. There are so many mentoring opportunities available to the executive that it is not difficult to capitalize on the important ones to make sure they are done well and that the benefits are achieved.

ORGANIZATIONAL DEVELOPMENT

While directing the overall development strategy of an organization, it can be tempting to get caught up in the latest business fad. However, I am firmly convinced that the best results come from consistently focusing on the business fundamentals. If the fundamentals aren't in place, then putting into play a new management strategy based on the current fad is not likely to achieve preferred results. Business fundamentals—the basic, proven business practices—are the foundation for achieving preferred business results. Mentoring the business fundamentals is the most likely way to produce preferred results. Drucker's *Managing for Results* is still one of my favorite sources for mentoring business fundamentals.

When I enter a company as the CEO, my objective is to assess the extent to which the business fundamentals are understood and applied. Frequently, I find deficiencies in both areas—the understanding and the application. One of the most productive activities an executive can undertake is to make sure his colleagues are sufficiently equipped with the fundamentals of business management so that they are aware of what "tools" they are expected to use. This can effectively be addressed in terms of identifying the core competencies managers need to have to be effective. Certainly, the requirements for the finance department would be different from those for the marketing department. However, the common core competencies are the fundamental management principles that our colleagues like Drucker have so effectively presented to the management profession. An annual review of Drucker's *Managing for Results* is time well-spent in just getting back to some of the basics on which a business is supposed to be focused. In almost every discipline I've encountered, basic reviews are appropriate.

Here's a chance for the executive to lead the mentoring process by seeing that this is done in his organization. And a post-evaluative session of these basic reviews always seems to produce positive responses.

CONTINUOUS MENTORING

The opportunities to mentor the team will expand as awareness does. The experience of successfully team-mentoring several situations will do that. I am always looking for ways to bring mentoring into play in day-to-day business activities. The more that mentoring becomes a way of life, woven into the fabric of the business, the more effective it becomes.

MENTOR'S CHECKUP

◇　Have you experienced the difference between being in a group and being on a team? What stood out as the major difference?

◇　For a moment, consider the Team Mentoring Objectives in Table 7-3. Can you imagine the impact these would have on a group in which you are a member?

◇　What approach would you use to bring Team Mentoring Objectives to your group? How would you sell it?

◇　Have you ever participated in or led team-development exercises? Is this something your organization does or could do?

CHAPTER EIGHT

MENTORING THE ORGANIZATIONAL CULTURE

OVERVIEW

Business culture has long been overlooked in terms of its impact on performance. Yet culture is the personality of the business, formed by the business leadership. This same personality creates the attitudes about most of what is important within the business. The successful businesses of tomorrow are beginning to strategize to create high-performance-oriented cultures.

This chapter addresses how the culture impacts business performance and how mentoring can strengthen the culture and enhance business results. Specifically, both healthy and unhealthy cultures are reviewed in terms of performance-inducing attitudes. The Six Principles for Exceptional Performance, introduced in Chapter Four, are evaluated in terms of their relationship to cultural values and performance. This then leads the reader to a cultural mentoring strategy to optimize the impact of the culture on business results.

An important part of the journey is an assessment of the kind of culture that currently exists. Then specific steps are presented on how to mentor the organization to create and sustain certain cultural values—values that will support exceptional performance.

LEADERSHIP IMPRINT

An organization's culture is a reflection of its CEO and senior management team. A look at the culture can provide a vivid image of what the senior management team models as their "walk." It is an imprint of the business leadership. With something as powerful as culture, it is surprising how little time and attention many senior management teams spend on developing the desired culture. Indeed, it is even more surprising how infrequently a strategy is developed to take advantage of the impact a high-performance-oriented culture can have. There *is* going to be a culture. And the culture is definitely going to have an impact on the organization's performance. So why not develop a specific cultural strategy to create an environment focused on exceptional performance?

——— ◇ ———

A look at the culture can provide a vivid image of what the senior management team models as their "walk." It is an imprint of the business leadership.

——— ◇ ———

Corporate culture is a reflection of the belief systems, values and practices of its management. And the chief protagonist is the CEO. Virtually the only way that culture-development occurs is if the CEO initiates it. The matter is too closely related to the CEO's persona for most managers to want to bring up the topic. To do so could easily come across as a move to change the CEO's behavior. Unless you are the CEO's spouse, that could be relatively risky.

Because the organization is and becomes what the culture supports, the senior managers are very much involved in the implementation of the culture. The soul of the culture emanates from the owner(s), entrepreneur, CEO, chairman or whomever is in the strongest position to guide the corporate beliefs, values and practices. Unless that person (or persons) sees the opportunity and shares the strategy for developing and implementing the culture, a less-than-significant result will occur. The big opportunity will be missed.

With such an opportunity to positively affect the spirit, personality and attitude of the organization, a definite strategy is called for. More often than not, it is benign neglect that keeps this subject from being addressed. It just hasn't occurred to the "culture drivers" that such potential exists. It's comparable to what is happening in so many homes these days. Many parents are not seizing the opportunity to help develop the best values and behaviors in their children. As a result, more and more young people are facing the issues of life without foundational preparation. No soapbox message intended, but the parallel seems clear. Attitudes and values *will* develop, whether we as leaders are involved or not. Why not go for the preferable option? Let's develop a specific strategy that will increase the likelihood of producing preferred results. And in line with the theme of this book, that strategy is best implemented through mentoring, and the CEO really is the driver.

CULTURE AND BUSINESS PERFORMANCE

The corporate culture has a significant impact on the attitudes of its members. Attitudes affect behavior, which then produce the business results. So the relationship between culture and business performance is significant. Various patterns of culture and performance relationships are identifiable. Considering the tremendous impact that an organization's culture—whether "healthy" or "unhealthy"—has on performance, a close look at what a strategy for creating culture can accomplish is warranted. But first we need to understand what makes a culture either healthy or unhealthy. The term "healthy" is used to describe a condition in which positive behaviors are produced that are supportive of and conducive to desired performance. Similarly, an unhealthy condition influences or produces behaviors that create less-than-desirable performances.

In 1992, two Harvard Business School-sponsored studies on the relationship between the business culture and the business performance of more than 200 firms were conducted by John Kotter and James Heskett. Their research and conclusions are described in their book, *Corporate Culture and Performance,* in which they conclude:

◇ Corporate culture can have a significant impact on a company's economic performance.

◇ Corporate culture will most likely become an even more important factor in the future in determining a company's success or failure.

◇ Cultures that can help organizations anticipate and adapt to change will be associated with superior performance over longer periods of time.

◇ Companies with more adaptive cultures strongly emphasize that managers throughout the business should provide leadership to initiate change in strategies and tactics to satisfy the interests of stockholders, customers and employees.

◇ It is not easy to change a corporate culture. It takes a specific strategy and strong leadership.

The single most visible factor that distinguishes major cultural changes that succeed from those that don't is competent leadership at the top. Culture then is really, really important to the business. It's a powerful force that in most cases exists with very little forethought about what can be done to improve it or make it more effective. But that is changing. The senior management teams of many businesses are beginning to realize the value of a strategy to create and support an effective culture. It just takes awareness and commitment. Consider now some of the aspects of a business' culture that can significantly impact performance.

UNHEALTHY CULTURES

There are certain business conditions that seem to nurture short-term actions or thinking. Under these conditions, the kind of management thinking that perpetuates a business has been given no priority and, as a result, no impetus exists to make it happen. Generally, the conditions present in an unhealthy culture are these:

◇ Strong centralized direction and decision-making

◇ Dominant market position

◇ Rapid success measured by growth and profits

◇ Insular management

Each of these is briefly discussed below.

Strong centralized direction and decision-making—This particular condition usually takes form through the persona of an entrepreneur. Often, it is supported by the size of the organization as well. The business strategy overall is that of a one-person show. Many successful businesses progress through this condition, but they are usually bucking the odds. The situation where one individual possesses the necessary vision and expertise to drive a business through several years of success is unusual. And such an accomplishment is becoming even more difficult in the knowledge age. Too many aspects of the business environment are changing too quickly for one individual to continually provide the best perspective. The process is just too limiting, or even risky, for a growing company to make sense of. It is too easy for the "unexpected" to deliver bad news.

Dominant market position—When a business is too successful, such as a company that is dominant in the market, a malaise can develop that weakens a business' preparedness. A couple of my CEO experiences came as a result of the prior management having become complacent in their success and, as a result, not being prepared for change when it came. Nothing in business lasts forever. But some managers behave as though their success is guaranteed, which makes their businesses quite vulnerable. At least twice a year management needs a "What's the worst that could happen?" meeting. A competent marketing department usually can have the agenda ready in short order for such a meeting. Fire drills are a good thing.

Rapid success measured by growth and profits—One of the risks of business success is the possibility of becoming lulled into complacency. This is a close cousin to the scenario described above. As Mae West said, "Too much of a good thing...is wonderful." But it is possible to become a bit too relaxed about the future. You should not be paranoid about the unknown. Just know that change is inevitable.

Insular management—This is a tough one. It isn't easy to tell someone they are out of touch. To the contrary, we all should be asking, "Am I in touch with reality inside as well as outside the business?" Other than in the case of a very small business, managing it rarely is a one-person job. A well-organized team with a strategy to stay up with change makes a lot more sense. Management without the ability to detect the forces of change early on will be blindsided. Not a healthy situation.

HEALTHY CULTURES

Healthy cultures promote healthy businesses. This is the "software" for long-term business success. A healthy culture promotes the kind of behavior that releases a force for excellence—and attracts the kind of people who create successful futures for themselves and the business. Company culture establishes the personality and attitudes that support excellence. And it's from this source of strength and focus that exceptional performance most likely will come.

As the CEO and the one person most responsible for the business' culture, my strategy has included the Six Principles for Exceptional Performance introduced in Chapter Four (Table 4-1). I continue to be impressed by how positive an impact these principles have on developing positive cultures or attitudes for excellence, which then contribute to exceptional performance. Let's consider them now in the context of the culture.

SIX PRINCIPLES FOR EXCEPTIONAL PERFORMANCE

1. Knowledge is power, hence, grow knowledge.
2. Leaders create results, hence, develop more leaders.
3. A state of harmony in the organization can more effectively release the full talent of individuals, hence, work on building harmonious relationships.
4. All development is self-development, hence, facilitate individual growth.
5. Knowledge workers work in small groups, hence, facilitate enhanced group-dynamic skills.
6. The organization's culture creates attitudes for excellence, hence, develop the culture.

Addressing the first five principles goes a long way toward achieving principle number six. To implement an effective strategy, consider mentoring culture at the three levels of human resource focus—the individual, the group/team and the entire organization.

—— ◇ ——

Healthy cultures promote healthy businesses. This is the "software" for long-term business success.

—— ◇ ——

Making a conscious decision to develop a specific culture is the all-important first step. Deciding that the culture can be an effective force in developing the organization's human resources will create benefits to the business and its members. Since the senior management team is very much an integral party of this process, their early buy-in and involvement is critical.

The cultural development strategy in Table 8-1 is an excerpt from the Strategic Mentoring Model (SMM) presented in Chapter Four. It presents the framework for mentoring culture. The greatest results and benefits for the organization and its individuals will be realized from the comprehensive implementation of the SMM. However, unless the culture is ready for it, the fullest benefit is unlikely to be realized. An organization's culture must be prepared for comprehensive mentoring in order to facilitate it most effectively. There must be congruency between the cultural ethos and the new practices introduced in the mentoring process. Consequently, that is where the CEO and the senior managers need to focus to properly design an implementation plan. An initial step is to assess the current state of the culture.

CULTURAL DEVELOPMENT STRATEGY

Individual	Group / Team	Organization
Facilitate developing individual relationship building skills	**Facilitate developing team relationship building skills**	**Facilitate a culture that emphasizes positive working relationships**
People create results, and people who work together accomplish even better results. Business usually requires people to work together for results. Therefore, effective people skills are an essential element of today's top business performers.	Groups that work well together have greater opportunity for achieving good results. Group success depends on building member relationships and drawing upon the abilities of all members.	People who work together effectively create better results. Working together effectively requires positive, supportive relationships. The organization's culture establishes the moral and ethical guidelines that create the character of the organization. The successful organization will manifest a culture built on character principles that produce excellence at all levels.

TABLE 8-1

ASSESSING THE CULTURE

A cultural assessment is a process of looking in. It can reveal some rather startling conclusions. Many conditions discovered in the assessment are the consequences of not having taken action or of not having made decisions regarding the desired outcomes. Nevertheless, results were created. There are numerous effects from passive decision-making. Your opportunity is to find as many "causes" as possible and evaluate how the effects can create improved results.

A cultural assessment team would benefit from a candid discussion about where this project is heading and what its goals are. This is the time to develop buy-in through designing the assessment process. Sensitive and effective leadership of this process is essential for best results. If the CEO and the senior managers can feel comfortable with it, this is a good opportunity to involve an outside, neutral facilitator, skilled in consensus development.

Here are a few questions that the team should consider in the assessment process:

◇ Where are you right now in your cultural development? What direction are you heading?

◇ What does a profile of your cultural values look like?

◇ How are these values reinforced by senior management?

◇ What values does the culture support and foster? How?

◇ What messages are being sent to your colleagues, informally as well as formally?

◇ What does your employee turnover tell you?

◇ Do your compensation and benefits plans match your belief system?

◇ What is your budget for training and development?

◇ Would your employees describe the company as a good place to work? What are exit interviews telling you?

◇ Are there discrepancies between your policies, your actions and your espoused belief system?

There are some fairly sensitive questions here that could result in some finger-pointing. However, that would prove counterproductive. The objective is not to find blame. Rather, the objective is to identify improvement opportunities, which is best done in a positive, encouraging atmosphere. The CEO can set the tone by reinforcing the good will and harmony of the process. The answers to these and other questions developed by the team should identify where to start working to improve the cultural elements that drive the business—the attitudes of those who create the business performance. This can contribute significantly to the agenda for mentoring the culture.

MENTORING CULTURE–SPECIFIC STEPS

There is no doubt that it takes numerous steps to mentor culture. I will share what I believe are some of the most effective ones. There is no particular order or priority. They are essentially common-sense moves to enlist the support of your colleagues to share in the commitment to produce excellence in the company's business results. The essential requirement is that the "troops" see and believe that this is what the leadership of the company truly embraces and practices. Most of it has to do with the manifestation of values, or truly walking the talk.

SPECIFIC MENTORING STEPS

a. Share what is important.

b. Communicate and model the belief system.

c. Encourage participation to empower change.

d. Be accessible and real.

e. Accentuate the "we."

When describing specific mentoring steps, I am addressing company leadership. Essentially, only the leadership can mentor the culture. So there needs to be a cohesive understanding and commitment to the methodology—the delivery system—in mentoring the culture. And I hasten to add, there is no one best way. These are guidelines for your consideration. Each of you must assess your own situations and develop the approach that works best in that setting.

Basic management concepts are transferable but the specific application *must* be sensitive to the particular setting. There is no cookie-cutter application. Each setting presents unique characteristics that will impact implementation. It's another example of the importance of knowing your customer or your audience.

A. SHARE WHAT IS IMPORTANT

One of my early memories of being really excited about my job, that is, being highly motivated and committed, was when my manager took the time to share important information with me. That communicated to me that I was important—important enough for management to bring me into the information loop, to be among the management group members who knew what was happening within the organization. I don't think I'm unique in that regard. Most everyone wants to be aware of things that are happening in their company that affect them.

People have tremendously inventive imaginations. If management creates or allows important information voids to develop, they will be filled! And usually by impressively creative imaginations. Unfortunately, the "void-filler" is usually wrong and possibly demoralizing to the troops, and then even more time and energy is required to undo the misinformation and get the accurate message across.

One of the most gratifying successes I have experienced in the process of creating new cultures occurred a few years ago when I assumed a CEO position in the United Kingdom. We had about 500 employees scattered among the countries of England, Scotland, France and Australia. Rumors were cresting as to what I was going to be doing in and to the organization. I countered this wave of anticipation over the next couple of months by hosting "tea parties." We would gather in small groups, usually in a conference room, serve tea and "biscuits" (cookies to all the Yanks) and have an informal chat. We got to know one another. I explained my background and what my mission was in the company—to help build a team of committed colleagues. And, to continue to build on the successes they already had created. I also shared the business objectives.

—— ◇ ——

If management creates or allows important information voids to develop, they will be filled! And usually by impressively creative imaginations.

—— ◇ ——

Through the process of inviting ten to fifteen employees at a time to have tea and discuss the mission ahead, and encouraging them to ask any question they wished, the information void was filled with meaningful information, and a relationship got off on the right foot. I encouraged them to tell me about a particular problem any of them had been experiencing that perhaps I could address and which would help them to be more effective. I knew this particular step could be risky and had to be handled very delicately. I certainly didn't want to pull the rug out from under their management by creating a "bypass" opportunity. I explained that any solutions would be discussed with their management and resolved however "we" effectively could. I further explained my mission was primarily to try to understand their situation and, hopefully, they mine. Actually their list of "needs" was pretty reasonable. Their managers and I tried to take quick action where possible to produce some immediate responses. Some quite positive outcomes resulted. One result that I was particularly striving for was trust. Not only from the troops, but from their managers and supervisors as well. It was a good process, and quite fruitful. And within the first three months of my tenure, this process fostered the building of positive relationships, based on trust, at all levels. I couldn't expect my colleagues to want to support my mission as their CEO unless and until they knew I cared about them. This is culture building.

The CEO has a tremendous opportunity to assure that effective communication is reaching the "doers." I have encountered many abysmal communication situations that just added debilitating "static" to the whole work process. It can deal serious damage to the business' culture. While the real costs are unmeasurable and unknowable, they are real and very, very significant to the overall efficiency and effectiveness of the business.

—— ◇ ——

Communication is difficult at best. And nothing less than a conscious, concerted effort to be really effective at it will support the drive for excellence in the culture.

—— ◇ ——

B. COMMUNICATE AND MODEL
THE BELIEF SYSTEM

By the "belief system," I mean the ethos you espouse about how you work together; that is, how you treat your customers, your suppliers, and your employees. If you say you believe in treating one another with dignity and respect, then it best be done. Period. To say one thing and do another takes the culture and performance downhill fast. The glue that binds the organization's culture to the motives supporting excellence is trust—trust based on a history of predictable fair play.

Perception has a tremendous impact on interpretation. Often just asking the question, "How is this going to be perceived?" will flush out the primary issues and concerns. If you wish your culture to reflect fairness and evenhandedness, regularly asking the question, "Are we?" will assist in maintaining those values. Keeping in touch with the troops (the workforce) in an open, approachable manner should keep the threshold of approachability low enough that the really important feedback will get through. However it is facilitated, a reality check is desirable from time-to-time. A candid report on how effectively you are modeling the belief system can be the basis for a valuable course correction. Or, at a minimum, it will identify opportunities on which to focus increased sensitivity.

A few years ago I encountered a company that proudly displayed their mission statement, which included a phrase about their commitment to their employees. Yet when a decision was made to remove someone from the organization, it was done in an extremely cold and near-cruel manner. Little, if any, concern for the individual's dignity was evident. The grossly insensitive way in which that situation was handled made a mockery of the company's mission statement.

It's best to not wave the flag if it's going to be trampled on. Oh sure, I understand bottom-line requirements. I've had to do more than my share of trimming. But it can and should be done with concern for others' dignity if you want to maintain a relationship of trust with the workforce and if your organization and its management inherently embody basic humane, ethical standards. Any possible savings created by a poorly handled cutback can quickly be consumed by the backlash reaction of the workforce, through various subtle and direct expressions of moral outrage directed at the company's apparent hypocrisy.

c. ENCOURAGE PARTICIPATION TO EMPOWER CHANGE

Nothing creates support like ownership. To the extent that broad-based involvement can be managed, change will be received and supported more positively. One of the most effective forms of involvement I have seen in an organization was when a particular company opened its financial performance data to the employees. This became the more objective scorecard by which all participants began to measure the company's behavior. When that can be achieved, then somehow linking employee compensation and/or rewards to the company's overall performance can have an even more potentially positive impact on building support.

The days of management keeping the company's financial performance "classified" and telling the employees just what to do, fortunately, is pretty much history.

This gets rid of a major contributor to the old "them-versus-us" mentality. And it releases the power of "we" and "my company." This is what this stuff we call "empowerment" is made: ownership creation. Not necessarily the kind of ownership that equates to stock ownership or interest, but ownership in the outcome. Doing what needs to be done to create exceptional results. Because you know "we" participated as "partners" in the process, these are "our" results. This has powerful potential, particularly as you consider the need in today's rapidly changing environment to be creative and vigilant in finding better methods to deliver better results. Harnessing and directing this powerful cultural attribute requires skill and finesse. And the payoff is a shared victory.

——— ◇ ———

The successful businesses of today are discovering the power of making the employees "performance partners."

——— ◇ ———

D. BEING ACCESSIBLE AND "REAL"

Organizations today are much flatter, or less traditionally hierarchical, which is a trend that is expected to continue. Over the past decade or so we have seen tremendous reduction in middle-management ranks. With the emergence of knowledge workers, who function best in small groups, less management is required. As mentioned earlier, businesses now depend more on *leading* knowledge workers because they manage themselves. So, flatter organizations work. Executive management just needs to make sure that positive, effective leadership replaces the reduction of the middle-management force.

Much has been written about the need for more leadership. But where is it coming from? Just because it now is needed, it doesn't necessarily follow that the upper echelon of managers can emerge as effective and powerful leaders. I believe this transition will occur in an effective manner only as the result of a well-thought-out strategy. Yes, that means a strategic plan for evolving to a more leadership-oriented "management" process.

At the heart of this transition will be the culture tenders—the CEO and senior management, the leadership structure—who must be accessible to the troops. This means *actually* being involved with them, knowing them, listening to them, nurturing them. Even taking criticism from them (constructive, of course!).

———— ◇ ————

Being "real" and not allowing position or rank to interfere with "partnering" with one's colleagues is crucial. Accessibility is a powerful contributor to building strong relationships based on commitment.

———— ◇ ————

Much can be accomplished in building a strong performance-enhancing culture by reducing the social and hierarchical distances between and among the players.

E. ACCENTUATE THE "WE"

There are some very tangible steps that can be taken to create a more supportive, "we"-oriented culture. I have touched on the power of the "we" but for the sake of clarity, just let me comment one more time on the need to reduce *differences* that don't make any difference. Homogeneity can be a contributor in building mutual commitment; the "we're-all-in-this-together" kind of thinking. It really does add a sense of camaraderie when it's genuine. Do you want a list? Okay. Here are the kind of things I believe are unnecessary in a corporate culture and which contribute to the "difference and distance" between the groups of players. They usually create more harm than good.

WAY AND MEANS THAT "DIFFERENCE AND DISTANCE" IS CREATED

⬦ Private bathrooms

⬦ Private dining rooms for executives only

⬦ Huge offices

⬦ Assigned parking for executives only

⬦ Associating/lunching only with peers

⬦ Disparate benefits

Now don't get me wrong. I understand the need to take care of the "heavy hitters"—the people who carry a big responsibility for achieving the business results. They must be well taken care of. But it doesn't need to be a visible perk that can create the wrong collegial message. Put the reward in the pay envelope where other people don't see it. It's getting difficult to do much else anyway because of tax consequences. And it will create more benefit for the business.

What are some positive "we" building activities? I can't produce the mother-of-all-lists for this one, but I can share a few activities that in my experience have been effective. Taking this list and challenging your management colleagues to double it would be a productive exercise. Here goes.

WAYS AND MEANS TO CREATE A SENSE OF COLLEGIALITY

⬦ Have lunch in the cafeteria/canteen/lunchroom at random with fellow employees.

◇ Host a monthly "coffee and what's happening" session (essentially to gain feedback) with a cross-section of employees. Mix it up each month.

◇ Host book discussion meetings with varying management representation.

◇ Minimize apparent differentiation between employee classifications.

◇ Make sure women and minorities are in management.

◇ Go to dinner with nonexecutives and their spouses.

◇ Have celebrations for major accomplishments.

◇ Look after colleagues who have "serious and unfortunate" circumstances befall them—show genuine "heart" (that presumably is heartfelt).

◇ Look for situations that create "fun" and encourage more of it.

◇ Have hallway chats with those you don't normally communicate with; i.e., the mail delivery person.

◇ Care

It's impossible to tell someone to "care" if it's not their nature to do so, however, I have found some profoundly sensitive and caring people in leadership positions. And I'm not surprised. I'm sure those traits served them well in the realization of their career potential. But sometimes we forget. With the mounting pressures related to keeping a business successful, sometimes the important gets shoved aside by the urgent. In culture-building, it's also urgent to do the important.

MENTORING THE STRATEGIC MENTORING MODEL

The biggest contribution to developing a performance-oriented culture is achieved through mentoring. The concept has been developed and discussed for the past seven chapters. I hope the material in this chapter has led you to a better understanding of the impact that culture has on performance. Culture is the spirit of the organization and it *can* be mentored.

Through mentoring, the attitudes for excellence can be woven into the very fabric of the organization's "being." By mentoring individuals, groups/teams and organizations, the foundation for the mentoring of culture will be in place. Then the question becomes, "What is it you want to mentor?" By mentoring continuous learning, leadership development at all levels, and relationship-building skills, a powerful human-resource-development process is unleashed. Development of people becomes the essential focus and the business' key resource. By adding the affirmation and reaffirmation of values that affect how we relate to each other, a strong performance-focused culture emerges—one that serves the individuals as well as the business. And that is the best kind.

Mentor's Checkup

◇ What type of performance do you think your business culture currently supports?

◇ Do you know how your company's employees feel about management's attitude toward them?

◇ What kind of feedback is the business leadership receiving from the employees?

◇ How would you describe the "trust level" in your organization?

◇ How effective are the communication processes in developing understanding and support throughout your company?

PART III

WHAT TO
MENTOR

CHAPTERS 9-11

CHAPTER NINE

MENTORING
A LEARNING
ORGANIZATION

OVERVIEW

Learning is at the heart of a dynamic, energized company. And that is what it will take to compete in the decade ahead. Chapter Two addressed the amount of change that is occurring in the business environment—it's daunting! What this means is that organizations have to change just to compete. In addition, competition also is growing. How do organizations change? They change through their people. And the focus of meaningful human-resource change should be based on learning.

Learning is one of the three major development areas utilized by companies that are focused on growth. Along with learning, the elements of the Strategic Mentoring Model include leading and relating. Even the mentoring elements of leading and relating, however, have a significant stake in learning. The expansion of one's leadership and relationship skills is grounded in expanded learning.

—— ◇ ——

The attainment of desired business goals requires a foundation in learning.

—— ◇ ——

Orchestrating learning is both challenging and rewarding, but there are lots of potential benefits in fostering a company-wide learning program. While there is a price to pay, the rewards are worth the investment.

The material in this chapter explores some of the key issues involved in emphasizing organizational learning. First, what comprises a *learning organization* is addressed. Then the strategy necessary to mentor an organization based on the concept of learning is introduced, followed by a description of the actual steps required to transform that strategy into reality. Learning is contagious and can be enjoyable. Organizations that have effectively implemented continuous learning strategies are creatively renewing themselves. And *that* is how to deal effectively with change and competition.

WHAT IS A LEARNING ORGANIZATION?

Learning is one of the key ingredients necessary for the achievement of exceptional performance. Learning, then, must become an ongoing process, so that renewal is a dynamic part of the culture. Peter Senge introduced the concept of a *learning organization* in his influential book, *The Fifth Discipline*, published in 1990. Essentially, a learning organization is one that has realized the importance of investing in the growth of its people—in a comprehensive way. Expertise from organizational-development professionals, who have thoughtfully evaluated precisely what a learning organization is, what it accomplishes and why one would pursue such a direction, is included.

WHY A LEARNING ORGANIZATION?

With so much happening in the world and in business specifically, it's becoming increasingly difficult to keep up. Change has become the companion, whether friendly or not, of every business. Businesses that learn to effectively deal with change—possibly even making it their ally—will be those that survive. As a result, preparing a company to compete and succeed in this environment requires an emphasis on learning.

KEEPING UP WITH CHANGE

In order for a business to survive and, it is hoped, to grow, it must maintain an understanding of what is going on in the general business environment. And it's becoming increasingly difficult for businesses to do that. Yet, businesses that have successfully incorporated a continuous learning and development process are those that are most capable of dealing with change. Since businesses are comprised of individuals, the process is based on continuous individual learning and development.

FUEL FOR THE ENGINE OF CREATIVITY

Have you noticed how university graduates come into an organization still enthusiastic to learn and ready to begin their careers? They have been involved in a learning process, acquiring knowledge that they are looking forward to using. Frequently, the realities of the workaday world dampen their spirits as the newly assimilated graduates quickly become part of the organizational fabric. And yet, the ones who somehow get on a fast-track are able to maintain their enthusiasm and spirit for learning. A close look at such individuals reveals that they are usually involved in some type of continuous learning process. Numerous studies have demonstrated that continuous learning fuels the engine of creativity. Wouldn't it be great to have this kind of resource constantly working for you? At all levels? Well, it's not out of your reach—but concentrated effort is required. Before getting into a discussion of the strategy of *how* to create a learning organization, it would be well to examine *what* creates a learning organization.

WHAT MAKES A LEARNING ORGANIZATION?

Peter Senge describes five "component technologies" that contribute to the creation of a learning organization. He explains that a major interdependency develops among these component technologies that enable organizations to become more productive. Let's examine them:

1. SYSTEMS THINKING

All of life seems to be tied together through patterns. Each has an influence on the rest, yet those relationships are not always seen. You can only understand this system by contemplating the whole process, which may depend on one's ability to think in broader terms. Business and other human endeavors also are systems. They are tied together by invisible lines of interrelated actions, which often escape your awareness. We tend to focus on isolated parts of the system and, as a result, don't quite figure out why the deepest problems never seem to get solved.

Systems thinking is a conceptual framework. It's a body of knowledge and tools that has been developed over the past fifty years to assist in making patterns clearer and to help us to see how to change them more effectively.

In newly formed organizations, particularly where management development has been underutilized, systems thinking probably will not be found in abundance. Young organizations, more often than not, grew under the influence of a strong entrepreneur. Entrepreneurial business strategies tend to take the form of project management more than systems thinking. However, developing a broader understanding of what systems can contribute to business performance provides significant payoff. It is essential to understand its application within the organization because of the probability that most *work* will cross departmental lines. Understanding systems supports a better understanding of how the work should be processed most effectively. Systems thinking is an essential part of the culture for the effective processing of work.

2. PERSONAL MASTERY

People who have a high level of personal mastery are able to consistently identify the results that matter to them most deeply. Personal mastery is the discipline of continually clarifying and deepening your personal vision, focusing on your energies, developing patience, and seeing reality as objectively as you can. This is an essential cornerstone of the learning organization—it is, in fact, the spiritual foundation of the learning organization.

The relationships between personal learning and organizational learning can then take the business on to greater achievements.

———— ◇ ————

It is interesting to observe the special spirit that develops in a business when it is comprised of learners.

———— ◇ ————

3. MENTAL MODELS

These are deeply ingrained assumptions, generalizations or even pictures or images that influence how you understand the world and how you take action, called *paradigms*. Paradigms are powerful because they create the lens through which you see the world. Your mental models or paradigms create your belief systems.

Quite often, you are not consciously aware of the effects your mental models have on your behavior. Many insights into business relationships are powerfully affected by your mental models. The discipline of working with mental models begins with turning the mirror inward. The ability to look at your internal pictures of the world and evaluate them in terms of how they are affecting your view of reality involves open thinking.

4. BUILDING SHARED VISION

This occurs as a result of leadership. It is very difficult for any organization to achieve greatness on an ongoing basis in the absence of shared goals, values and commitment. When there is a genuine vision (not just a vision statement) people excel and learn, not because they are told to, but because they want to. Shared visions galvanize an organization toward exceptional performance.

The practice of shared vision involves the skills of evaluating and analyzing shared "pictures of the future" that support genuine commitment and enrollment rather than mere compliance.

5. TEAM LEARNING

One of the most exasperating situations in the management world is to observe how a team of committed managers with individual IQ's above 120 can function with a collective IQ of 65. Yet it happens—it happens when people cannot work together effectively.

Teams do need to learn how to work effectively together. You know that teams can learn. You have seen it in sports, the performing arts, the sciences and, yes, even occasionally in business. In business, when the intelligence of the team exceeds the intelligence of the individuals, extraordinary results are created. Peter Senge states that the discipline of learning starts with "dialogue," which is the capacity of team members to suspend assumptions and enter into a genuine place of "thinking together."

―――― ◇ ――――

When the intelligence of the team exceeds the intelligence of the individuals, extraordinary results are created.

―――― ◇ ――――

The discipline of dialogue also involves learning how to recognize the patterns of team interaction that undermine learning. The patterns of defensiveness are often deeply ingrained in the way a team operates. If unrecognized, they can undermine learning. So the task of creating positive learning environments for teams involves focusing on the activities that produce positive interaction and dialogue, which involves mentoring team learning. Team learning is vital because teams are the fundamental learning unit in modern organizations.

STRATEGY FOR MENTORING A LEARNING ORGANIZATION

MANAGEMENT MENTORING

The five disciplines described above function as an "ensemble" to support the learning organization. In order for a business to become a learning organization, genuine focus is required, as is the case in other disciplines. To practice a discipline is to be a life-long learner within that discipline. Applied specifically to learning, continuous acquisition of knowledge by members of the work team is the goal. Enriched by expanded knowledge, exceptional results occur when people learn to effectively apply the knowledge together, to trust one another's support and concern for the overall success of the team—and for the individuals who form the team.

Where does the leadership come from to support this type of organizational discipline? The chief executive certainly has a major influence on the culture within which such a phenomenon can flourish. However, the most powerful strategy is for the entire management team to seize this opportunity and create the cultural discipline to sustain a learning focus.

Now to return to the thesis of this book. Imagine the power created by the management team who is mentoring those within the organization in the five component technologies identified by Peter Senge and then expanded by the likes of Stephen Covey, Peter Drucker, Warren Bennis, Daniel Tobin, Daniel Goleman, Robert Bennett... and the list goes on. I've had the privilege of sitting in a room with a group of managers and leading them in a discussion about personal mastery and the impact on their own abilities to manage, the power of the team, the impact of a shared vision—and I can tell you that it's not only exciting, it's powerful.

Mentors essentially are guides. Guiding managers to take on knowledge that facilitates transformed thinking is a responsibility of the CEO and his senior managers. This is also true for every manager.

Having seen the opportunity and become determined to act on it, facilitation of the process is next. Let's go back to the Strategic Mentoring Model. Your strategy is to mentor learning at three levels: to the individual, to the group/team and to the organization. Following, in Table 9-1, is the summary strategy for mentoring a learning organization.

STRATEGY FOR MENTORING A LEARNING ORGANIZATION

Individual	Group / Team	Organization
Facilitate continuous individual learning	Facilitate continuous learning of team-excellence building	Facilitate the development of organization-wide learning
As the basic building block of performance, individual learning involves a commitment to self-mastery and a continuous quest for knowledge. As conducting a successful business becomes increasingly knowledge-based (knowledge is power), the importance of individual learning is paramount.	Working groups provide the advantage of collective knowledge and skills that may be used in achieving a goal. Especially effective are groups that also begin to learn together from sources within and outside the group.	Knowledge and information are critical commodities of the future. Future success is much more likely when continuous learning becomes an integral part of the culture of an organization.

TABLE 9-1

To implement this strategy effectively, specific implementation action is required at the individual, team and overall organizational levels. The point is that all three levels need to be addressed to achieve the full realization and impact of learning. This is how it becomes culture.

Mentoring A Learning Organization

Management Focus

There is a fundamental responsibility for the senior management team that basically translates to running a profitable business. This requires constant readiness. As change expands dramatically and competition becomes more pervasive, business in general is becoming more difficult. The major business publications constantly provide readers with enormous amounts of information on changing markets. Business in general is not just evolving, it's exploding. As business managers, what do we do to cope with all the uncertainty? Look to your people. Invest in them to meet the compounding challenges.

Exceptional Financial Results

By all definitions, the main responsibility of the chief executive is to produce the leadership and management discipline to create the preferred financial results. Without equivocation or doubt, that is number one. An executive can create all kinds of wonderful people programs and motivational strategies, but if it gets in the way of achieving the preferred bottom line results, then problems will certainly develop. The development of a learning organization should be supportive of this primary objective. In fact, a company without a commitment to develop its people, one that drives its human resources only for bottom-line results, may indeed do very well in the short term. My comments, however, are directed toward maintaining a balanced approach to preferred bottom-line results, as well as building a renewal element into the engine of the business.

RENEWAL

Most senior managers have been caught up in using their human resources to achieve short-term results and not in giving sufficient attention to improving the delivery system, which is their people. Business pressures regularly result in managers looking after the urgent while neglecting the important. It's a familiar trap in business and in life. However, a well-managed business can do both if properly focused, and by doing both will achieve better results.

Several businesses I have dealt with or been a part of have had senior level managers espousing continuous learning. However, if such pronouncements are not actively supported by the chief executive, they will lack the necessary impetus to become broadly embraced and practiced. Certainly, the chief executive has enough to look after. Yet, he really needs to be proactively involved in spreading the gospel, emphasizing the importance of the company's involvement in continuous learning and development—and he needs to model it. When the CEO models behavior, it becomes culture.

OUTSIDE ASSISTANCE

So what does a CEO do if he is not prepared to be a mentor? Not every chief executive or senior level manager is necessarily interested in doing it or even has the skills. It is advantageous to have the chief executive visible and active in the mentoring process. The truth may be, however, that the chief executive just isn't equipped to do the job. What to do then? Mentoring is important enough to an organization that outside assistance should be engaged to make sure that such a process occurs. And I quickly add that the right specialist or consultant to help facilitate this process should be someone who has experienced a variety of management situations. The chief executive must be cautious in bringing in outsiders to do this. There needs to be a good "fit" and an effective strategy. Having an outsider visibly involved does not carry the same impact as having the chief executive as sponsor. An outside specialist/consultant, however, may well advise the chief executive on how to lead a mentoring program with the executive as the visible leader. It may be a jointly designed program with much of the architecture coming from the consultant. However, the visible leadership needs to be the CEO and senior management.

Having been in organizations where development impetus came from the top, I have seen some fairly impressive results. There needs to be specific strategic objectives for the program or it tends to wander. Even efforts that are not focused can create some desirable benefits. However, so much more can be accomplished with a thoughtful strategy that has milestones along the way to measure benefit. This calls for a comprehensive implementation strategy.

FOCUSED LEARNING

Most learning is beneficial. However, some categories of learning will have more immediate business benefit. The business will be rewarded most by a targeted approach to continuous learning. I propose four learning areas, and a strategic mentoring plan for each:

1. CORE COMPETENCIES

First of all, competency can be described as a package of skills and technologies, rather than a specific skill or business process capability. For example, a core competency of McDonald's is to provide food of consistent quality at any one of their worldwide locations. This involves massive systems development, logistics, training and inspection. The core competence of the Federal Express Corporation is packaging and delivery based on various skills and technologies, including bar-coding, communication, network management, and linear programming, to name a few. It is this integration of skills that produces the core competence.

———— ◇ ————

Maintaining high levels of competence in competitive markets means keeping core competencies finely honed.

———— ◇ ————

Competition between and among businesses essentially is based on the matching of core competencies. How does Company A stack up against Company B in its perform-ance? How good are they at their core competencies? To compete at the highest level, an organization should develop a mentoring strategy to achieve championship performance levels in their core competencies. Have you ever heard of McDonald's Hamburger University? Com-panies competing at world class levels must have world class people-development programs or they won't stay in the game.

Maintaining high levels of competence in competitive markets means keeping core competencies finely honed. A mentoring strategy to perpetuate peak performance in core competencies is a significant management opportu-nity. Following are five steps that management should undertake to maintain leadership in its core competen-cies:

◇ Identify existing core competencies

◇ Establish a core competence training and develop-ment program

◇ Build core competencies

◇ Measure and evaluate core competencies

◇ Continually improve core competencies

Each business has knowledge unique to its industry. Being a leader in that sector seemingly would involve being a knowledge leader as well. The question that high achievers ask a lot is: "What else can I do?" This really works well with learning. The exciting thing about putting a championship team together is observing the way most champions think, which is along the lines of "What else can I do?" That's what makes them champs. Believe me, leading champions is a lot more fun than having to "jump start" the troops to get them to do what is good for them and good for the company. Self-starters, work leaders, champions, whatever they may be called, should have the desire, agenda, or strategy to be at the leading edge of their particular knowledge specialty.

2. BUSINESS FUNDAMENTALS

Critical knowledge for any person bearing the title *manager* includes a good working grasp of what I call the business fundamentals. I have found no better description than what Peter Drucker identified in his book, *Managing for Results.* He introduced the following eight points, which are *the* business fundamentals.

a. *Neither results nor resources exist inside the business.* Both exist outside. Drucker goes on to say that the one and only distinct resource of any business is knowledge. Other resources, such as money or physical equipment, do not confer any distinction. What does make a business distinct is its unique resource, its ability to use knowledge of all kinds. It is only in respect to knowledge that a business can be distinct.

b. *Results are obtained by exploiting opportunities, not by solving problems.* All one can hope to get by solving a problem is to restore normality. True results come from exploitation of opportunities.

c. *Resources, to produce results, must be allocated to opportunities rather than problems.* Needless to say, one cannot shrug off all problems, but they can and should be placed in proper prospective.

d. *Economic results are earned only by leadership, not by mere competence.* Profits are the rewards of making a unique, or at least a distinct, contribution in a meaningful area; and what is meaningful is decided by both market and customer. Profit can only be earned by providing something the market accepts as valuable and is willing to pay for as such.

e. *Any leadership position is transitory and likely to be short-lived.* No business is ever secure in its leadership position.

f. *What exists is getting old.* Most managers spend their time on the problems of yesterday. It's almost futile to restore normality, which is only the reality of yesterday. Your job is to change the business, its behavior, its attitudes, its expectations, as well as its products, markets and processes to fit the new realities.

g. *What exists is likely to be misallocated.* It is dangerously tempting to keep on patching yesterday's garments, rather than work on designing tomorrow's pattern. Often those areas that get the least amount of attention are those that really produce the results for the company. Managers should look for patterns of the Pareto Principle—20 percent of the customers provide 80 percent of the results, or 80 percent of the problems are attributable to 20 percent of the processes—look for distinctions and significance.

h. *Concentration is the key to economic results.* Economic results require that managers concentrate their efforts on the smallest number of products, product lines, services, customers, markets, distributive channels, end uses and so on, that will produce the largest amount of revenue.

The fundamentals—the business basics—need to be renewed on a scheduled basis; that is, renewed in the sense that people need to revisit them in a way that keeps the concepts fresh and makes them a part of everyday working practices. This practice of renewal provides a great setting for mentoring. A continual emphasis on the improvement of business fundamentals can establish an ongoing dialogue among managers that provides new-found opportunities to improve the business.

3. LEADERSHIP

Growing businesses need leadership at all levels. In the next chapter leadership-mentoring strategies are developed. At this point, I will mention a couple of thoughts about leadership that pertain to the overall learning agenda. The first step in developing potential leaders is to teach them about leadership. This requires that (1) they gain an understanding of the qualities and characteristics of a leader and (2) they also learn what it is that a leader does to provide leadership.

Much has been written about leadership development, the necessity of having leaders at all levels of an organization, and the importance of shared leadership through team management. Also, the number of leadership development seminars available in the marketplace has been impressive. However, having poked around quite a few businesses, I'm continually impressed with the opportunity that still exists to cultivate leadership. Take a look at the leadership development that really is occurring in your organization. Come on now, I mean *really* happening, with *real* leadership skills being developed and deployed. My assessment of the successful companies in which I have had the opportunity to become intimately involved (rather than only casually acquainted) is that they know how to develop leaders and leadership—and are doing it.

4. RELATIONSHIP SKILLS

The fourth learning priority I commend is the building of awareness and competence in relationship skills. I develop this subject more fully in Chapter Eleven, particularly as an integral element of the Strategic Mentoring Model. Here I want to emphasize its importance in a focused learning-and-development program. A conversation with most human resource professionals will confirm that this is the most troublesome area in personnel management. Getting people to work together in harmony increases the quality and quantity of the output. And the work can be a lot more enjoyable. So shouldn't you be learning a lot more about this subject, and how to be better at it? Particularly since relationships permeate the entire business and create the "conduit" through which work flows (or doesn't)?

The mentoring of learning, leadership and relationship-building creates a dynamic synergy. Mentoring leadership development starts with self-leadership. Leaders want to be effective. Being effective requires knowledge, so leaders want to do what is necessary to acquire knowledge. Combining leadership and knowledge development will point leaders toward effective relationships, a requirement of working through others, which leadership entails. A pretty remarkable synergy and a tremendous benefit from mentoring.

MANAGEMENT FOCUS

As our environment becomes more complex, human beings have developed an exceptional ability to forget about the things we should be doing. In the process of dealing with the constant demands made on our time in the work environment, it is easy for the important issues to be displaced by the urgent. Unless a definite strategy is in place to review the *important;* i.e., to identify the progress being made on the important projects and programs, they can easily get pushed aside. This takes leadership—and the chief executive is just the person to provide it. A nice way of dealing with this opportunity is to make it a regular part of a program for improvement and transformation; to revisit your core strategies on a regular basis. The mentoring culture supports this approach nicely, but it needs someone at the helm to make sure that the focus is on the key strategies and the business fundamentals.

There are a number of activities available to the chief executive, the department heads or other senior managers to provide vehicles for learning. Keeping one's staff focused on growth and looking for better ways to achieve business results is extremely healthy. I like to compare it to the physical workouts and scrimmages that we see professional sports teams employ when preparing for competitive challenges. As energized business managers, why shouldn't we be doing the same?

A few years ago I hired a department head to manage a department that had underachieved significantly and definitely needed a refined work-measurement system. In conjunction with coaching work-measurement, it's helpful to have a manager demonstrate how it is being accomplished. In this case, I had the new department head spend several months improving the work-measurement system and then had her present it at one of the executive staff meetings. Let's call her Mary. Here were some of the benefits Mary created:

a. She knew she was going to be judged by her peers on the quality of the presentation as well as the content. She gave it the highest priority.

b. In the process, she created a work-measurement system, which went through several incarnations involving discussions with me, the group finance director, and the marketing director. The result was quite thorough.

c. It reemphasized to the other department heads the importance of having good measurement systems in place. And it gave them an opportunity to view the quality of the work as well as provide feedback.

d. Hopefully, they were challenged to continue to refine their own work-measurement systems to obtain the best possible results.

e. The process embodied *gravitas*—that is, it reinforced the importance of work measurement in this culture.

THE CONSUMMATE RENEWAL SYSTEM

The beauty of having a dynamic and comprehensive mentoring system at work in your organization is that it enables the renewal of your most valuable asset—your people. Volumes have been written about the benefits of having a high-quality, motivated human resource energetically attacking the company's objectives. After considering the alternatives, this seems to be one that can make a rather significant contribution to achievement of that number one responsibility constantly faced by management—profitability.

MENTOR'S CHECKUP

◇ What role does learning have in your organization? How widespread is it? Who drives it?

◇ How does your personal growth strategy impact your personal leadership?

◇ To what extent is your organization cultivating and developing its core competencies?

◇ What is the greatest learning opportunity in your organization? Has it been identified and is it being addressed?

CHAPTER TEN

MENTORING LEADERS AND DEVELOPING VISION

OVERVIEW

The future of business is in its leadership. That's not so profound. What is profound is the fact that the fastest-growing businesses utilize shared leadership. By that I mean decentralized, broad-based leadership. In fact, a new term is being popularized in the business environment—*workleader*. Recent studies have revealed that in successful organizations, certain patterns of leadership are being repeated—every leader works and every worker leads, thus, the term *workleader*. The trend reflects a growing reliance on empowerment and participation in the business processes, with leadership occurring at all levels.

Where is this leadership coming from? Essentially, it is being developed from within—home-grown leadership. With the downsizing of mid-management structures, leadership vacuums created by this shrinkage are being filled by workers at all levels. In addition, teams are becoming more integral in work processing, providing management direction for processes under their direction. In short, there is a leadership revolution, and more leaders are needed.

The strategy that will field leadership effectively throughout the organization is mentoring. Leadership needs to be developed at three levels—the individual, the team, and the organization as a whole. The material in this chapter presents a strategic approach for developing leadership throughout the organization that will facilitate exceptional performance. Leadership is one of the three essential elements of the Strategic Mentoring Model. Organizations that implement this strategy will be able to effectively manage change and prepare for growth.

PERSPECTIVE ON LEADERSHIP

Leadership has been an interest of mine since my college days. My first leadership-development experience occurred during my undergraduate studies in a class called "Leaders and Leadership." This was in 1959. Since then, I have collected vast amounts of literature on the subject, held numerous leadership positions, taught and lectured, consulted, observed...and wondered. I am fascinated by it.

My conclusions about the importance of leadership in achieving exceptional results have emerged as the result of being in the "laboratory" of real business application, augmented by continuous study of the subject. No, it didn't take me thirty years to become convinced.

Fortunately, that happened somewhere early on. Experience has intensified my belief in the importance of leadership. Ultimately, what has emerged is my Strategic Mentoring Model, which holds leadership as one of the key ingredients of exceptional performance. It is significant that learning and human relation skills usually accompany leadership and performance capabilities.

Exercising the right kind of leadership at the appropriate time makes such a difference to the outcome of an endeavor—whether it is running a multinational company, organizing a new product launch, or running the annual community charitable drive. Or even organizing a retirement dinner. Organizations endowed with people who can exercise creative resourcefulness develop followership along the way. And this kind of leadership can be mentored throughout the organization, creating an exceptional resource to enable a business to create exceptional results.

I can safely say that those of you who are reading this material are exercising a form of leadership. The interesting thing is that most leadership occurs without awareness that it is happening. Carrying out your roles as managers, husbands, wives, fathers, mothers, or, in fact, almost any role, creates leadership situations. The extent to which we create the best possible results is dependent on how well we fulfill those leadership roles.

The more you understand what leadership is and how to develop and deploy it in your business, the more prepared you will be to meet the challenges you face in the increasingly competitive business environment. Through leadership mentoring, businesses can be better prepared to achieve higher levels of success. This requires a specific strategy. As a part of developing this strategy it is productive to first review what we as managers have learned about leadership in the last few years.

LEADERSHIP EXAMINED

The generally accepted management-leadership distinction of recent years is attributed to Peter Drucker and Warren Bennis, who explain that *management means doing things right and leadership means doing the right things.* The successful enterprise must embrace them both: leader-managers who can identify the right things to do and then do them right.

Leadership often is evaluated in terms of the qualities one observes in leaders. Some of these qualities, such as intelligence, energy and enthusiasm, are easier to identify than others. John Adair, a leadership specialist in the United Kingdom, defines a leader as "the kind of person with the appropriate knowledge and skill to lead a group to achieve its ends *willingly.*" By comparison, the manager is responsible for managing the enterprise. The processes used to achieve the desired end represent the definition of management. Many managers meticulously carry out their management responsibilities while exercising very little leadership. Conversely, there are excellent examples of leaders who know very little about the process of management. Almost all elected officials would fall into this category. They were not elected for their management expertise, but rather for their leadership abilities.

In examining leadership, I wanted to develop a definition that included more than just what leaders do, but also what they create and how they create. Leaders see opportunities to create results and they seize them. They ask, "What else can I do?" They proactively look for ways to achieve exceptional performance. These features need to be considered when it comes to what is being mentored. So, here is my definition of leadership:

Leadership occurs when individuals anticipate and identify an opportunity to make something positive happen, and then take responsibility for the process and its results. Leadership creates followership. Followership occurs when the leader offers a trustworthy direction.

PATTERNS OF LEADERSHIP

In 1985 Warren Bennis and Burt Nanus published an influential, landmark book titled *Leaders—The Strategies for Taking Charge.* Their findings were based on original, in-depth analyses of ninety top leaders—executives at companies like GM, Arco and Lever Brothers, as well as senators, governors, labor leaders, orchestral conductors, film producers, college presidents and athletic coaches. Bennis and Nanus reported numerous and varying patterns of management and leadership style. In fact, there seemed to be no obvious patterns for success.

They began their project by examining how power is used in the organization. They concluded that power is the *reciprocal* of leadership. There are several well-known examples of the combination of power and leadership— with Lee Iacocca no doubt topping the list. But these are the unusual manifestations of unique leadership. They wanted to document the kind of leadership you can learn from and infuse into your organizations, at all levels.

The Bennis-Nanus research revealed similarities in *leadership behavior.* All ninety of the leaders embodied four groups of competencies from which four patterns were identified. They are vision, communication, trust and self-management.

1. VISION

Management of attention through vision creates *focus.* All ninety leaders interviewed had an agenda—that is, a clear goal in mind. This led Bennis and Nanus to conclude that leaders are the most results-oriented individuals in the world, and results are what get attention. Visions or intentions are compelling and pull people toward them. Intensity coupled with commitment is magnetic. Also noted was the fact that leadership is a transaction between leaders and followers. Neither can exist without the other. Leaders bring out the best in those around them. They create unity by bringing all the players together to focus on results.

Working with visionaries is an interesting experience. Visionaries may create unity in their direct support group but they often face opposition as well. Creation of unity by the decision-makers, the people who have direct influence, fosters common direction and common focus—and ultimately, exceptional results.

——— ◇ ———

Leaders are the most results-oriented individuals in the world, and results are what get attention.

——— ◇ ———

Back in the mid-seventies I had the opportunity to serve as director of management services under newly elected Portland, Oregon mayor Neil Goldschmidt (who was only 29!). Neil had a passion for mass transportation. He was upset with the concept of urban sprawl created by the proliferation of freeways. He made it a priority to push for urban mass transit. But the impact of his personal vision was not merely confined to the area of Portland. His vision for a transportation system eventually led to his appointment as secretary of transportation under President Jimmy Carter. Several years later, Neil became governor of Oregon where again his vision provided focus for creative direction.

A visit to Portland today reveals a beautiful riverfront city and a vital downtown area with exclusive bus grids, a light rail system that is still expanding and a metropolitan area that has come to grips with mass transit. Sure, Portland has its problems just like any other big city. Yet I could certainly point to a lot of other cities that haven't come close to solving their problems as well as Portland has. And what made it possible was one individual's *attention through vision.* Certainly, there were lots of other leaders involved; Neil doesn't get all the credit, but he certainly was one of the leaders whose vision provided the focused energy necessary to create a better future. The results speak of his vision.

2. COMMUNICATION

Shared vision has provided the stimulus for many organizations to go beyond the accomplishments of the ordinary. Leaders are able to articulate the vision and communicate the feelings that attract colleagues towards goals. People generally will not support a particular program, direction or concept until they understand it. Sure, blind allegiance is given to charismatic leaders. But we don't see as much blind allegiance in the business environment as we do in the political environment. The unforgiving demands of the marketplace soon render this leadership style ineffective and inappropriate.

For long-term success, organizations depend on the existence of shared meanings and common understanding of results, which facilitate coordinated action. Leaders articulate and define what has previously remained implicit or unsaid. An essential factor in leadership is the capacity to influence and *organize meaning* for the members of the organization.

Finally, the distinctive function of leadership is to maintain a quest to "know why" rather than to provide "know-how." This is the primary difference between leaders and managers. Communication creates meaning for people; it is the only way any group can become aligned behind the goals of the organization, and the only way one can realistically develop support and commitment from others. Getting the message across at every level is essential to achieving the results you need in today's business climate.

3. TRUST

Trust is the lubricant that makes it possible for organizations to work. Without trust, you cannot develop support from those with whom you work. The process of developing trust is not to be taken lightly; trust is something that is earned. Further, you trust people who are predictable and make their positions known. Trust is the underlying issue not only in getting people on your side, but in having them remain there. There are four ingredients that leaders must have to generate and sustain trust:

a. *Constancy*—Whatever surprises that leaders themselves may face, they should not create them for the group. The team just does not like surprises. Good communication will maintain that trust.

b. *Congruity*—For leaders, there is no disparity between the principles they espouse and the lives they lead. Leaders walk their talk.

c. *Reliability*—Leaders are there when it counts. They are ready to support their co-workers in the moments that matter.

d. *Integrity*—Leaders honor their commitments and promises. You can depend on them.

When all four of these factors are in place, people are willing to give them their trust and support. The chief objective of leadership is the creation of a community of workers held together by a common purpose. Organizations and their leaders inevitably have to deal with the basic needs of people, which is why values, commitments, convictions, even passions, are basic elements in any organization. Since leaders deal with people, not things, leadership without values, commitment and conviction can only be empty and ineffective.

4. SELF-MANAGEMENT

One of the more interesting discoveries made during the Bennis-Nanus interviews was the importance of human-relation skills in leadership. They found that the higher the rank, the more interpersonal and human the undertaking. They found that a key factor in interpersonal effectiveness is self-management.

Without self-management, leaders may do more harm than good. If we can't manage ourselves, how can we possibly lead and manage others? In this complex business age, the management process has become more voluntary on the part of the managed. If you really want to achieve exceptional results, then those who are managed need to feel ownership of the goals. This occurs more often when self-fulfillment is a vital element of the work processes. A positive self-regard is the result of nurturing skills and discipline; that is, the ability to continue working on and developing one's talents and abilities.

Your individual potential is a direct result of your self-esteem. If we don't feel good about ourselves, then to expect very much from ourselves is difficult.

LEADERSHIP BEHAVIOR

Wherever I have observed exceptional performance in an organization it has been accompanied by a valued companion, leadership. In some organizations, there may be only a few standout, individual leader-performers, but usually in highly productive environments, leadership is pervasive. Fortunately, leadership skills can be developed. Some people may be gifted from birth with special skills and intelligence that have enabled them to develop more easily into effective leaders. And some people are fortunate to have been raised in family settings that have nurtured many of the personality qualities and characteristics that facilitate leadership. Others have been exposed to role models and encouraged in growth activities that yielded leadership traits. However, since leadership is becoming such an important aspect of business performance, more leaders are needed at all levels. And that is precisely what managers of organizations who are seeking to optimize their human-resource performance should be doing; developing leadership at all levels.

Developing leadership capabilities that can be deployed throughout an organization is a significant undertaking. What specifically would be the focus of such a development exercise? A comprehensive study on multi-level leadership titled *Leadership IQ* adds additional support and clarity to the content of this book. E.C. Murphy, Ltd., an international research and consulting firm specializing in leadership development, produced a study by Emmett Murphy of the beliefs and practices of more than 18,000 leaders in 562 organizations, including healthcare, public service organizations and other businesses over a five-year period. All sorts of organizational settings were involved. What emerged were patterns that were repeated from one setting to another. What they learned was that in successful organizations, *every leader works and every worker leads.* Outstanding leadership situations were found at every organizational level, from warehouse clerk to CEO. From this observation, the authors coined the term *workleader,* which emphasizes the important relationship between work and leadership.

The Murphy research also identified what it is that leaders seem to know how to do. The behaviors of those in the study were evaluated and patterns of know-how or actions that contributed to high performance were observed. Here is what the workleaders in the study did:

◇ *Selected good people*–They knew both how to screen and how to hire effective people, as well as how to help them maintain their effectiveness.

◇ *Focused on the right cause*–In the day-to-day work environment it's easy to be diverted from the main mission. They knew how to stay focused on the priority activities.

◇ *Solved problems that arose*–They had the confidence and know-how to maintain work momentum when a "snag" came along. They dealt with it and kept processes moving.

◇ *Evaluated progress toward objectives*–They knew where they were going and what steps were necessary. Then progress was tracked to assure the desired results would be realized.

◇ *Negotiated resolutions to conflict*–They understood the debilitating nature of conflict and worked to resolve differences positively.

◇ *Reduced trauma created by change*–They recognized the causes of uncertainty and performance-lowering behavior caused by change. They addressed the changes to create understanding and support.

◇ *Protected the culture from crises*–First of all, they understood the culture and it's importance to attitudes and performance.

They could recognize the negative influences and effectively deal with them.

◇ *Synergize worker efforts*—Essentially this was team-building and leading. The power of the team was realized by building common focus and commitment.

These are the performance behaviors of workleaders. Their belief systems and convictions (character, if you will) motivated them to behave in ways that created followership. Not blind followership, but enlightened and collegial support to get the best results. This is what you want to understand how to develop—so you can then mentor it.

MENTORING LEADERSHIP

Awareness of the foregoing information, hopefully, has helped developed a broader appreciation for the impact of leadership on overall performance. Exceptional performance can be facilitated through enlightened leadership, functioning at all levels. Having empowered *workleaders* throughout the business is powerful and can add the essential ingredient to facilitate change while supporting growth.

How does an organization develop this type of leadership and performance phenomena? I am convinced it can be mentored, just like a sports team can be coached to greatness. While the analogy is a good one, the major difference in the business setting is the diverse and varied activities that need to be focused; and the diverse and varied backgrounds of the participants. Yet a comprehensive mentoring strategy can provide the impetus for diversities to become strengths in an empowering, performance-oriented culture. *Mentoring leaders throughout the organization to identify opportunities and take responsibility for results is the enabling process.*

The steps necessary to create this process involve mentoring leadership at three levels: the individual, the group/team and the organization/culture. The Strategic Mentoring Model includes the leadership function as shown in Table 10-1, which highlights the three-tiered process.

STRATEGY FOR MENTORING LEADERSHIP

Individual	Group/Team	Organization
Facilitate individual leadership development	**Facilitate team leadership development**	**Facilitate the development of leadership at all levels**
Leadership occurs when individuals identify an opportunity to make something positive happen, and then take responsibility for the results. Followership, the essential companion, occurs when the leader offers a trustworthy direction. The best strategy for creating followership is to provide a model that others will follow.	Many successful businesses are led by small teams that may be found at any level within the management hierarchy. Increasing team leadership capabilities helps create even more internal resources that can be used toward achieving good business results.	Cultivating leadership at all levels is one of the most effective success strategies. Supporting and cultivating leaders to take responsibility will provide the necessary resources for tomorrow's challenges. Leaders should serve as models while carrying out the corporate strategy.

TABLE 10-1

Implementation of this strategy begins with mentoring individual leadership development. The first step is to help the individuals understand where they are in their leadership development and to identify specifically what they wish to develop. The next step in the progression of comprehensive leadership development involves mentoring the team. The third step is to mentor the organization, which really means to mentor the culture in terms of developing the attitudes that support the exercise of leadership at all levels. The culture has a tremendous impact on the realization of leadership development overall. Specific leadership mentoring strategies for individuals, teams and the culture follow.

MENTORING LEADERSHIP TO INDIVIDUALS

Recognizing opportunities and taking positive action is what leaders do. The culture has a lot to do with whether this actually happens. Spotting an opportunity, then seizing it and taking responsibility for creating a preferred result, is most likely to happen when it is encouraged and supported by the culture. The most inhibiting—or supportive—influence (depending on perspective) comes from the top. To develop the broad usage of leadership in an organization, you first must ensure that the culture is supportive.

In a couple of my CEO positions, I have followed very strong entrepreneurs. Strong in the sense that they were the epicenter for leadership and decision-making. As a result, little independent initiative had been developed elsewhere. In one setting the primary stockholder had been the entrepreneur-founder of that very successful business. He was still on the board and active in the business when I was recruited. His brilliance and focus-for-results had created an impressively successful business. But sustained growth required an experienced CEO, which accounted for why I was brought on the scene. The biggest hurdle in moving the organization into a framework and culture of participative management, along the lines I have been describing, was the legacy of a single strong leader; we'll call him Bill.

Bill was so successful at calling the shots, from Day One of the company's start-up, that it became the norm. No one thought of making decisions independently of Bill. In fact, much of the thinking had to do with "What does Bill want done on this one?" This worked fine when the organization was small but became increasingly difficult for Bill to keep up with as the business grew. Thus, on my arrival, in addition to finding an exhausted

Bill, I found a management team that was under-experienced and underdeveloped in decision-making skills and, naturally, leadership. A major cultural shift first had to occur to enable the development of leadership capacity, and its eventual implementation. Just launching leadership development without the attendant cultural development would have been ineffective. I relate this to underscore the importance of a business culture that supports a change of direction.

In this scenario, the executive team first had to be introduced to an entirely new way of thinking about how the business was to be run. They were about to have a much more involved role. Their jobs were changing. Their responsibilities were being broadened. Were they ready? In a word, no. Oh, they were excited about the opportunity to participate at a higher level in the management of the business. However, when considering the need for experienced know-how, there was a definite void. They just had not previously been called upon to develop and use these resources. But now it had become necessary to catch up.

For the first six months, I concentrated on developing and mentoring the culture, as well as mentoring several of the executives. Again, I want to stress the fact that changing a culture is not a short-term endeavor. Of course it depends on how significant the necessary changes may be. The key is to get the senior management team on board as supportive participants in the process. Unfortunately, the transition required changing a couple of the players. The "distance" or amount of change necessary to achieve the needed level of performance was too great for some who subsequently had to be replaced. This was necessary for the good of the team, the business and the individuals who were replaced. And it was an essential move to carry out the strategy of creating empowered leadership throughout the organization. Competent leaders need to be the models.

What gets rewarded gets developed. On the one hand, if management says they want to see a much broader application of leadership in their organization, but they don't "reward" it when it is achieved, be prepared to be underwhelmed.

―――― ◇ ――――

Too much control can stifle the kind of initiative that can produce exceptional performance.

―――― ◇ ――――

The next critical ingredient in the leadership-development process is trust. To increase the use of leadership, leaders and potential leaders have to know that it's okay to take some risks. I'm not talking about the kind of risks that could ruin the company. It has more to do with the freedom and confidence necessary to make decisions. To grow leadership, decision-making needs to be dispersed. Decisions need to be made at the lowest possible level in the organization where the best knowledge and judgment can be applied. That's how you advance the people and the business.

I cannot recall the many times I have encountered senior managers who were still making decisions that rightfully belonged with a subordinate. Maintaining "control" often drives managers to perform mundane tasks that should be systematized into a process handled at a lower level. There are still too many managers with unclear thinking about control. Too much control can stifle the kind of initiative that can produce exceptional performance. The emphasis must be on results, rather than control of the process to achieve the best outcomes. It is the ends, not necessarily the means, that need emphasis. Sure, judgment must be applied so that the correct, even the best, means are used. The very best processes are desired and should be continuously "tweaked" to make them the best. Management needs to provide clarity on the desired outcomes and then encourage the *workleaders* to employ the best means to achieve them.

So, mentoring more workleaders is a significant opportunity. Here are four positive actions to pursue in mentoring leadership.

1. TEACHING

To expand the leadership base, understanding should be developed on two levels. First, strive to provide clarity on the desired outcomes, the "what." There needs to be understanding in order to build support and commitment. Then, the "how" can more effectively be developed. There are seven principles that will support the development of leadership behavior. Understanding and applying these principles will enable more workers to become workleaders.

a. *Achievement*—Knowledge is an essential ingredient for self-reliance and personal competence. And both are prerequisites for achievement. Achievement will support the development of followership. Followers are attracted to achievement. What you know and what can be accomplished with that knowledge supports the "workleader" role.

b. *Pragmatism*—A realistic and common-sense approach to work is what most often produces the best results. Making sense of the day-to-day work-flow offers a workleader the opportunity to create rational processes that continue long after the need that created them has disappeared. Noticing and seizing improvement opportunities differentiates the workleader from the mere worker.

c. *Customer Focus*—An intense commitment to provide exceptional service is an invaluable achievement attribute. Understanding the role of a "customer-partner" can be the catalyst for excellence. Also, recognizing the internal customer, that is, the next person in the process, is a crucial part of a quality-oriented culture.

d. *Commitment*—Leaders cannot easily be deflected from their convictions if they are to be effective. A tenacious, yet sensitive, commitment to see that things are done properly, at the highest quality level, creates exceptional results. Maintaining allegiance to a vision, a goal or objective is an essential ingredient for its realization.

e. *Optimism*—Seeing possibilities is difficult to do if you allow problems to get on top of you. Transforming difficult situations into opportunities starts with the proper attitude. And the maintenance of a "can do" philosophy is rooted in optimism. Also, this is reflective of confidence developed through successes in similar circumstances.

f. *Responsibility*—Accepting responsibility is the first step in creating results. To achieve the results that people most desire requires that they accept personal responsibility. And it can't be delegated. Leaders recognize the opportunities and accept personal responsibility for the achievement of results.

g. *Humility*—Readily acknowledging that one doesn't have all or most of the answers is an invitation for participation. Leaders facilitate relationships with people who want to help them be successful. This is another form of followership developed through creating an attractive model.

A personal understanding of these seven leadership principles is a very important step in assessing where to start the mentoring process. Potential leaders need to know what creates leaders, what leaders do and then conclude what they each personally need to do to become a leader or improve their leadership abilities. *Then* the mentoring can begin.

The mentor should guide the mentee through a discussion of each principle, jointly assessing the extent to which the mentee has mastered the concept as well as the practice. At this point, awareness is the key objective. Awareness should be followed by a process of making the principles second-nature for the mentor.

2. MODELING

As mentioned earlier, setting the example by modeling the specific behavior is one of the most effective means of teaching and reinforcing a principle. This is particularly true when the organization's leadership, the CEO and senior management, are the models. They are the models in establishing the culture that drives the business performance. Then they should mentor their "direct reports" to do the same. Learning about a leadership culture is new and exciting to most innovative people who have gone through the entrepreneurial stages of centralized leadership and decision-making. And there will be a learning curve to go through. Modeling the desired behaviors is effective in helping the mentees/learners catch on more quickly to the opportunity by being able to see what the preferred behaviors look like.

As a strategy, modeling works best when guided and assessed by senior management. They need to be on the lookout for examples of the specific behavior being modeled. When observed, it is most productive to call attention to it in a discreet way so as not to embarrass the model. A positive reinforcement technique is to catch someone doing something right and sensitively issuing an "Attaboy."

3. COACHING

In Chapter One, I explained the distinction I make between mentoring and coaching. Mentoring is broad-based guidance in overall development, while coaching is more target-specific. Coaching specific skill development and setting up exercises for growth provide support and enable establishment of the mentoring strategy. I use coaching as a "subset" of mentoring. But I don't want to put too much emphasis on the labels—essentially, you are involved in human resource development. The important point is to *just do it.*

Coaching leadership usually involves one-on-one assessment and feedback sessions. The coach really needs to understand the seven principles discussed above and to be able to assess the quality of their application. Coaching human behavior in an organizational context is not a task for the novice. The person being coached must be seeking growth in order for this to produce the best results. And to be the most effective, the method in which the coaching is delivered needs to be sensitized to the audience; that is, the individual personality. Entire books have been written on this process. It's sufficient for your purposes here to urge that the coach:

◇ Be practiced in assessing performance and providing feedback.

◇ Give thought to making the feedback constructive and positive.

◇ Be an excellent model, and if in doubt, ask his boss.

4. REINFORCING

Policy and cultural reinforcement need to come from the top and, most important, it must be modeled. The most effective reinforcement is to observe the company leadership modeling the preferred behaviors. Period. Yes, it's a daunting matter. It's an awesome opportunity and responsibility. But as one of my colleagues says, "That's why they get the big bucks."

The more that senior management can be involved in teaching and coaching leadership, the greater the impact in reinforcing it throughout the organization. Effectively increasing individual leadership capabilities throughout the organization requires development and training. A specific development strategy to enable leadership training at all levels can be a reinforcing message to the workforce. Knowing management is allocating budget resources to develop leadership skills communicates a definite commitment.

MENTORING LEADERSHIP TO TEAMS

As a result of more work now being accomplished by teams, increasing their effectiveness is a desirable business objective. I like to keep an eye on the newspaper advertisements to see what the current market conditions are. Recently, I have noticed most high-tech companies include in their employment ads a statement to the effect that applicants "must be able to work effectively in small groups." In knowledge-based businesses, which seem to be the ones that are proliferating, working in small groups or teams is the norm.

First, we need to understand what it means to be a team. Mentoring of teams involves training, modeling and reinforcing effective team behavior.

Many successful businesses are led by small teams. Teams that provide distinct leadership may be found at any level in the management hierarchy. Increasing team-leadership capabilities helps create even more internal resources that can be used to achieve exceptional business results.

———— ◇ ————

A small group is not necessarily a team. Until there is real cohesiveness and mutual commitment, it remains a small group.

———— ◇ ————

I have had the privilege of developing several very effective executive teams. In preparing this material, I reviewed some of the specific tactics I used in the process. Immediately after assuming responsibility for the executive staff or "small group" (I can't assume they are a team yet), I held a "team definition" meeting in which I acquainted my prospective team members with my S-I-L-E-C-T team leadership strategy.

a. *Support*—Each member of the team must support the other members in whatever form is necessary to achieve the team goals.

b. *Initiative*—The success of the team depends on each member taking initiative for results. The "good ideas" need to bubble up, not be handed down.

c. *Loyalty*—Each member of the team needs to know his back is safe. If there is a problem, it gets resolved between the specific team members who are having the problem; the matter doesn't get subjected to third party reviews.

c. *Empathy*—If one of us hurts, we all hurt. If one team member has a problem, then we all do. You need to

understand where your teammates are operating from—
their biggest problems and their biggest opportunities.
Then you can contribute.

e. *Commitment*—Commitment to the team members
and the team goals needs to be modeled. A cohesive
executive team does much to build confidence in the
business leadership.

f. *Trust*—Trust is the glue that holds all relationships
together. It's to be protected like the crown jewels.
Building trust in the organization is one of the significant
leadership opportunities of the executive team. Trust is
one of the most far-reaching attributes of the team, as well
as of executive leadership.

—— ◇ ——

Without trust there is no relationship or followership.

—— ◇ ——

Mentoring the team leadership strategy (SILECT) to
the executive team is my job as CEO. Each team has its
accountability manager—and that's the person who should
do the mentoring. It is unfortunate that the team function
often is handed over to a group (I have seen this happen
endless times). And the group never progresses to the
point of functioning as a team. A huge opportunity is
missed. And very little leadership develops. Oh, once in
awhile there may be an enlightened soul in the group who
can rescue a situation like this. But far better results can
be realized from a distinct team/leadership-development
strategy, rather than by leaving to chance some rather
significant opportunities.

Mentoring team leadership also can occur as specific
mentoring activities. One of the more effective methods I
have found is the book discussion group. Select a

particularly cogent book, or article, on some interesting and applicable aspect of leadership. Review it together and draw conclusions regarding application and benefit. It can be a very productive team-mentoring activity, as well as relationship-building endeavor, which certainly strengthens the team.

A creative mentor can no doubt think of numerous other settings in which to model and continue to develop the understanding of team dynamics and team leadership. The business itself offers the most effective settings in which to capture learning opportunities. A proactive attitude toward developing team leadership will create numerous opportunities to mentor.

MENTORING LEADERSHIP TO THE CULTURE

Cultivating leadership at all levels is one of the most effective success strategies. Supporting and cultivating leaders to take responsibility for results builds the resource that will carry businesses into the next century. The culture is truly a reflection of the CEO's leadership style. The values and ethics of the culture are a reflection of his leadership. And that ethos impacts every work attitude in the house.

Often attempts are made at addressing the corporate ethos in a mission statement. Yet I have seen some tremendous "value violations" of corporate mission statements. To espouse one policy and execute another is a real shortcut to the destruction of trust. Without trust, you have no support for performance. Low trust equates to low performance in just about every business setting I have ever seen.

——— ◇ ———

The values and ethics of the culture are
a reflection of its leadership.

——— ◇ ———

The CEO is responsible for protecting the culture from value violations. And just as important, the CEO also provides leadership for a culture that supports empowerment of the work force to excel. Perhaps more than any other writer, Tom Peters has documented some outstanding cases that indicate what empowered work forces can accomplish. His description of supportive cultures reveals the presence of powerful, enabling forces that create performance focus. Not to mentor the culture to create performance-oriented values is to ignore a significant opportunity for better business results.

Having inherited some fairly unproductive cultures, I have had to go through some rather laborious rebuilding processes. Building and sustaining cultures that recognize human value and emphasize fair play and excellence has worked very well for me, my colleagues and the businesses I have managed. Here are some of the values I have mentored in the process either of establishing, or reestablishing, a high performance-oriented culture. This is by no means "the list" to go by. Rather, it is simply what has worked for me. Many of you may be able to add to it and improve upon it.

a. *Executive Missionaries*–This is not a one-person job. I want the executive staff to be in sync with me to create a seamless model. So, the first thing to do is to ensure that the SILECT team strategy is in place. You must function as a team, not only to achieve your best business purposes, but to create and nurture your culture as well. You are the culture creators and sustainers. Your mission is to create the best culture you can to support your business objectives and your work colleagues. Creating a company of "winners" is based on commitment to a win/win ethos.

b. *Honesty*—I have always been a little bothered when someone says "To tell the truth..." and then tells me something. Do they not tell the truth the rest of the time? Even some of the time? As a leader, my character must support trust. The temptation to shade the truth is sometimes powerful. With some people it seems to be a disease—and once they are so labeled, credibility takes a hike. Leaders must be known for their trustworthiness.

c. *Integrity*—Maintaining integrity essentially means to do as you say. It's knowing the right thing to do...then doing it—consistently. Taking shortcuts is not allowed. I have pointedly counseled my colleagues to please, please bring to my attention the slightest drift in my performance from what I espoused as my credo. Effective team members can do that for each other.

d. *Harmony*—Friction among team members is like throwing sand into the engine crankcase. It is so wearing. This is not to say disagreement is out. Good debates with passion are wonderful generators of better ideas and direction. But the process shouldn't turn sour. Keep relationships positive; the subject matter can be heated but after the scrimmage, we are all on the same team. Friction in relationships is debilitating to ongoing cooperation, focus, energy and commitment. Problems have to be fixed. Cultivate harmony for creative, energized relationships.

e. *Dignity and Respect*—This is how we treat one another. There are no exceptions. It doesn't matter whether it involves hiring or firing someone. There can be no other way to treat people and expect trust to be part of your culture.

f. *Communication*—I have always thought this is a good way to let people know how much you really appreciate them—by how much you communicate with them. What kind of a job you do in keeping people informed and "in the know" is a tip-off to how you value them and the relationship. People want to know what is going on in their company. It usually is not intentional, but so many companies keep too much information in the "inner circles," thus allowing the rumor mill to fill the information voids. There is a better way. Treat people like colleagues and they will work like colleagues.

g. *Open the Books*—People need to know what they are working for and how their company is doing generally. That is, if you really want to develop support and commitment. Sharing important financial performance information spreads the gospel, "We're all in this together." Otherwise, you risk encouraging the "them" and "us" syndrome and also miss out on the opportunity to develop a "partnering" mentality. You want to work on developing the power of "we."

h. *Invest in People*—Take a look at your human resources development budget. What does it tell you? Helping your prime resource develop is a great investment. I was fortunate enough to have my graduate degree paid for by my employer. I was impressed, appreciative and my contribution to the enterprise undoubtedly was enhanced. It was a big deal to me and strengthened my commitment to my job as well as to continued growth. And I don't think I'm too different from anyone else. That kind of investment becomes a win/win proposition.

i. *Care*—I have always wanted my company to be a company with heart. People need to know they are important and you can let them know in so many little ways. I enjoy sending birthday cards to all the employees.

I know there is a difference when you are dealing with thousands rather than hundreds. But the thousands need to seem like hundreds and the hundreds like dozens. Personalize when possible. Look after the bereaved family, send flowers to the new mom. And let the community know you care too. In my last company, we had hundreds of volunteers participating in events with our chosen community service (handicapped children). Such involvement is a great contributor to "community" within your company as well as outside of it.

j. *Bad Apple Policy*—Yes, there are some people you just can't afford to have on your team. You can't lower your standards, so people who can't meet them need to go play in someone else's ball game. To keep the person in the company who violates one of your ethical tenets could signal that "it's okay" or that you don't take this stuff as seriously as you say you do. This point should not be taken lightly. Deal with each case with dignity and respect.

k. *Accountability*—This had to come up sometime. Ultimately we all have a responsibility to add value to the business process. After all, that's what we managers are paid to do. The more the contribution can be measured the more the fog factor is removed. Once again, "If you can't measure it, you can't manage it." You need to be able to determine the return-on-investment, generally, from top to bottom. That is just good stewardship.

l. *Have Fun*—This one gets overlooked a lot. I'm a big fan of celebrations. When major milestones are achieved, recognize the contributors and celebrate. Everyone needs a little recognition and appreciation. Celebratory events, discreetly planned and executed, can be very positive culture builders.

◇ ◇ ◇

Well, there they are. At least twelve ways to build a culture that enhances leadership development. Each CEO will want to add his own flavor. The key is to have a strategy and an assessment process to determine whether it is being realized.

Leadership development has been one of the most enjoyable aspects of my career. Seeing people grow, take on more responsibility, create more results, and achieve new successes, has all been exciting and rewarding. And, everyone benefited.

MENTOR'S CHECKUP

◇   What is the decision-making climate in your organization? Is the culture supportive of dispersed decision-making? How can the process be enhanced?

◇   Are you a part of a work team? Describe the trust level. How about harmony? Do you notice any relationship?

◇   What is the most important thing you can do to enhance your leadership skills? How is your progress?

◇   What can you do to be a more effective mentor of leadership?

CHAPTER ELEVEN

RELATING–MENTORING RELATIONSHIP SKILLS

OVERVIEW

Positive relationships bind people together to enable exceptional performance. Effective relationships are no accident. When they exist, look for individuals who possess some of the most important skills in the business environment. The ability to work together effectively is what releases potentially unused human-resource ability. Just think of the impact of having unused ability mobilized because of improved relationships. Fortunately, human-relationship skills can be developed.

There is a strategic approach for nurturing positive relationships. The objective is to mentor the proliferation of workleaders who model relationship skills. Company-wide training coupled with mentoring and modeling will help develop individuals, teams, and a culture steeped in knowledge and the practice of effective social skills. More creativity and productivity result when the culture and its people are attuned, thus creating a harmonious, energized work force.

THE IMPORTANCE OF WORKING TOGETHER

With the recent emphasis on the work group, many companies are now screening for applicants who have effective human-relation skills. Discussions with my colleagues in the management-recruiting business reaffirm the emphasis being placed on interpersonal skills. And this emphasis is happening at all levels, not just in executive management. The ability to work effectively together is essential in the age of the knowledge worker. People who work effectively together can facilitate the participation of all the contributors to the process. To do otherwise may be cutting off valuable contributions that are "shut down" by an environment less supportive of participation. Career success increasingly is influenced by a person's effectiveness in using relationship skills.

One of my CEO responsibilities has been to assess relationship-building skills for two purposes. First, all things being equal, I want to build around people who can effectively enable a collaborative work process. My experience solidly supports the conclusion that more effective results emanate from "work process centers" with a pro-collaboration orientation than those struggling with relationship problems.

Further, colleagues who are less effective in using relationship skills should be focused on developing these skills. The process can range from reorientation and education, to one-on-one coaching to professional counseling. So, this may get complicated along the way. The human personality is multifaceted, complex and not easily changed. However, a significant opportunity exits to help create an awareness of the importance of specific behaviors. Then, if the individual can reach inside and produce these behaviors, great! My experience has not always ended with the outcomes I have desired. There have been both victories and failures, as one would expect. But it is responsible stewardship to try. More often than not, the task is not so much the creation of a new behavior as the cessation of annoying or unproductive behavior. The process usually involves enabling the individual to see and comprehend the "unproductive" behavior and be challenged to consider the consequences of its continuation. Thus, an understanding of the dynamics of human behavior is becoming essential in the workplace.

UNDERSTANDING HUMAN BEHAVIOR

For senior managers, having a working understanding of human behavior is becoming more important in order for them to be effective management practitioners and mentors. Being able to identify behaviors that produce "performance static" can lead to effective mentoring and coaching that may not otherwise occur.

All behavior is motivated. Mentors and coaches must build relationships to uncover those conscious and subconscious motivators that keep people stuck in old patterns of behaving. Modeling the behavior as a mentor clearly articulates the desired behavior and the need for it as it relates to business results. The sole purpose of this process is to increase effectiveness at all levels. If overall performance can be made more effective by eliminating influences that diminish effectiveness, then workleaders need to become more skilled in identifying and coaching these "opportunities." This is a strategy that supports building a business that can function in an internationally competitive environment in which success is measured by fractional differences among companies, products, markets, skills, profits and performance.

Assessing Performance

Assessing the performance of management personnel increasingly involves evaluation of human interactive skills. Observation of the behavior of successful managers often discloses a high level of practiced behavioral strategies, which produce preferred results. In Chapters Four and Ten, the characteristics of successful manager-leaders were discussed. These characteristics are the result of certain behaviors that have created success for them and, as a result, became their characteristic behavior styles. There's a pattern here. Essentially, that is what is being observed in human behavior—patterns that tend to produce consistent results. Understanding these patterns is of great—if not essential—value as a mentor. Following is a discussion of several approaches to identifying styles of human interaction.

Styles of Human Interaction

Most executives do not have the benefit of extensive formal training in human behavior. A working under-standing of the fundamentals, however, can provide us with better insight on how to deal with various kinds of behavior. These principles have proven to be most helpful in generally understanding that there are certain personality types—and that if you can tailor your mentoring to their particular behavioral styles, then you are likely to have greater success. Acceptance of the concept of behavioral styles hinges on acknowledging that people are not totally unpredictable. In fact, based on research, repetition of activities and situations occurs as people develop habitual ways of dealing with their environment. This way of viewing human interaction began in 1924 with Carl G. Jung's research on psychological types. Significant research and use of Jung's model has produced several enriched applications of Jung's ideas. In particular, the Meyers-Briggs Type Indicator (MBTI) is a widely respected tool for identifying personality type. Jung's four types are as follows:

1. *Thinker*–Organized, structured, accurate, research-oriented

2. *Sensor*–Active, concerned with results, goal-oriented

3. *Intuitive*–Imaginative, impetuous, stimulating

4. *Feeler*–Emotional, spontaneous, introspective

Jung's model asserts that dominant and auxiliary preferences we depend on in adult life develop in childhood and adolescence.

Throughout childhood and adolescence, people develop behavioral styles based on what has created the best successes for them. There are many more complex psychological issues behind this that we don't need to delve into at this point. Let's proceed on the basis that, indeed, there are specific, identifiable behavioral types. And, the more you can understand the differences and their effects on relationships, the more you shall be able to use this knowledge to effectively guide the mentoring process.

Behavior patterns that people develop, that create acceptable results for them, generally become habitual. Hence, people are somewhat predictable because they behave habitually. When people function in social situations they exhibit observable behaviors that help to define their particular behavioral styles.

BEHAVIORAL STYLES

Managers need a process, a convention, to identify certain behavior styles to facilitate examination and discussion of their implications. Behavior is the manifestation of such personal elements as character, beliefs, personality, knowledge, emotions—potentially complex material. Getting heavily involved in personality and behavior analysis, for which few of us are qualified, would most likely be counterproductive. However, you do need to at least understand behavior and its implications in a manner that supports the mentoring process. Having a model to facilitate this process is helpful.

Phillip Hunsaker and Anthony Alesandra have developed a practical set of guidelines to evaluate behavior types that work very well in the management environment. In their book, *The Art of Managing People,* they identify behavioral styles according to two primary characteristics—assertiveness and responsiveness. Behavior indicative of these characteristics is recognized by the verbal, vocal and visual behaviors of people. In this behavioral style model, *assertiveness* is defined as the amount of control one person tries to exert over other people and the situation. It is seen as the amount of forcefulness a person uses to express his thoughts, feelings and emotions in an effort to influence other people. To assist with your behavioral style assessment, assertive behavior is further divided into either *high assertiveness* or *low assertiveness.* Table 11-1 shows frequently used descriptions of behavior for both low- and high-assertiveness types. Certainly every manifestation of assertiveness will not be on one of these lists, but it provides an idea of the range of manifestations of assertiveness. For this purpose, let us consider the range of behaviors.

ASSERTIVENESS DESCRIPTIONS

Low Assertiveness	High Assertiveness
Quiet	Verbose
Mild opinions	Strong opinions
Avoids risks	Takes risks
Meditative decision-making	Swift decision-making
Pleasing first impression	Powerful first impression
Shy	Active
Reserved	Confident
Supportive	Confronting
Easygoing	Impatient
Slow actions	Fast actions
Listens	Talks

TABLE 11-1

The second dimension of behavioral styles that you want to examine is *responsiveness*. This refers to the readiness with which a person expresses emotions and develops relationships. Similarly, responsive behavior is divided into high-responsiveness and low-responsiveness. The range of manifestations of this style are listed in Table 11-2.

Professors Hunsaker and Alesandra combined these two scales into four quadrants that divide assertive and responsive behavior into four different patterns referred to as behavioral styles (Table 11-3). The name of each of the styles (*amiable, expressive, analytical, driving*) represents its general characteristics. It is interesting to note that these styles are quite similar to Jung's *feeler, intuitive, thinker,* and *sensor* styles. An individual's style of behavior is not a complete profile of his personality or character. Typically, personality instruments *do not* measure values, emotional maturity, intelligence or actual skills. But in mentoring that individual, it's an effective way to describe the manner in which that person interacts with others in the social and work situation.

RESPONSIVENESS DESCRIPTIONS

Low Responsiveness	High Responsiveness
Aloof	Personable
Formal and proper	Relaxed and warm
Fact-oriented	Opinion-oriented
Guarded	Open
Controlled	Dramatic
Disciplined	Flexible
Task-oriented	Relationship-oriented
Hides personal feelings	Shares personal feelings
Thinking-oriented	Feeling-oriented

TABLE 1 1-2

The Hunsaker/Alesandra research is a good source for further evaluating how best to assess these behavioral styles and understand the model. A basic understanding of these human-behavior patterns prepares the mentor to more effectively deal with the process of mentoring different personality or behavioral styles.

FOUR BEHAVIOR STYLES

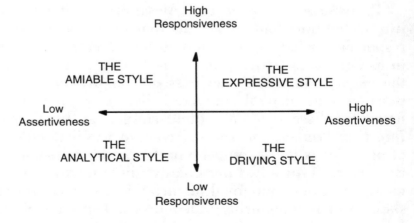

TABLE 1 1-3

Just as management strategies need to be varied from one business to another, likewise mentoring strategies need to be tailored to the particular mentee's behavioral style. Understanding the differences can increase the effectiveness of your specific approach to those being mentored.

This serves as a good model or guide, but it's not a substitute for your own judgment in terms of how to assess these behaviors. As a mentor becomes familiar with a mentee's particular behavioral styles, this helps put these behaviors in some type of context. It provides better understanding of the implications of the various manifestations of these behaviors. Also, knowledge of the model helps assess what type of performance usually can be expected. For example, in a particular setting where management may prefer someone with the expressive style to drive for the results needed in a very strategic project, it would probably be a mistake to appoint someone who has more of an analytical style. We all have preferences, which make given behaviors more of a natural strength, but we can learn other necessary skill competencies in order to function effectively as leaders. At least the model is useful in stimulating awareness that there are predictable results from certain behavioral styles. This fact needs to be considered, whether mentoring, hiring or counseling.

One of the greatest benefits of this material is that it can assist the mentor in evaluating the mentee's potential performance. A significant amount of the mentor's evaluation of the mentee is based on behavioral observation. Having a convention or process that he can use to build a dialogue with the mentee can prove most helpful. This model can be used to explain certain behavioral assumptions the mentor is making and to open a dialogue with the mentee. The model also can be useful for exploring the basis of the mentor's assessment. So much of the mentoring process is based on asking questions and considering options. This could give rise to such questions as, "What consequences are you likely to experience as a result of your behavioral style concerning this particular assignment?" Then one would need to make sure that the behavioral style being attributed to the mentee is truly understood according to the model.

Unless some type of convention is established for carrying on a meaningful discussion, in which both parties are using the same terminology with mutual understanding of its meaning, communication will be difficult. Within a broader growth strategy, the model can support discussion about usual results of various behavioral styles. Prompting mentees to articulate their goals and their objectives, and what they will feel comfortable doing, is a productive part of the process. A mentor would not want to be guiding the amiable or analytical types into high pressure, driving situations for which they would be mismatched. A discussion at the inception of these processes, which can raise awareness of such situations, is strongly suggested.

This model was helpful to me a few years ago when I was in the process of reviewing the performance of a vice-president of business development. In general, his job was to identify, analyze and recommend potential business acquisitions for the company. He was a terrific guy, well-liked by everyone. He had a superb education—the right schools, the right graduate degree—a very impressive package. But he couldn't "close." He couldn't bring a project to fruition. His research was terrific but the business really had nothing to show for it. In one of our regular meetings, I asked "Bill" to describe, from his perspective, the implications of his performance on the business, as well as his career. We agreed that his analytical and amiable styles were pleasant to work with. However, in terms of the assertiveness needed to create the results we were looking for, it just didn't seem to be there. After several sessions, all quite friendly and fairly unemotional, we concluded Bill just didn't have the one essential element in his performance portfolio that would enable him to bring a project to fruition. He then understood more clearly that we had a problem. We mutually agreed that he would be better off in a more research-oriented environment than one in which so much depended on the specific results he created. Both of us would be much happier.

Bill is still a friend; we correspond from time to time— but he's in a much less stressful situation where his research is appreciated for what it is. We used a model similar to the one discussed above to evaluate characteristics of individuals with various behavioral styles. We jointly recognized that there was not the best fit in this situation and we were able to develop a reasonable strategy that worked. The model was a good facilitator and took some of the pain out of the personal interactions. I wasn't focusing on Bill; I was focusing on his performance within the context of this particular model. I did not attack him; we addressed the issue that we jointly identified. Interestingly, Bill said he had tried numerous self-help strategies to address this particular situation, but had not found anything that helped him achieve that result. I was appreciative of such a model to help facilitate this process with Bill, while simultaneously maintaining his dignity and his friendship. The way these matters are handled gets factored into the impression by other senior personnel of how the "culture" deals with these problems. Fairness and dignity are essential in supporting a highly developed performance culture.

SOCIAL COMPETENCE

Much has appeared in the business press during the past decade regarding the impact of social skills on career success. Let's face it, the manager's job is to get work accomplished through people. Having the social skills to do that effectively is essential to the job. As his career progresses, a manager's technical competencies become less important, while his social skills become increasingly more important. The social arts, the "people skills," are competencies that make for effectiveness in dealing with others. Deficits in these competencies lead to ineptness or repeated interpersonal problems. It is the lack of these skills that can cause even the intellectually brilliant to founder in their relationships. While this may not destroy the career of a manager, it certainly can impact his effectiveness and future career advancement. These social abilities allow one to shape and encourage a relationship and to mobilize and inspire others to work together effectively. They are the skills an effective manager must have.

Yet I am seriously disappointed in the level of effort I see in most companies to strengthen these skills. Hey, the old bottom line requires a lot of focus, for sure. But investing in people is equivalent to investing in the system that creates the bottom line. Neglecting one of the most important opportunities to "rev up" the corporate engine just doesn't make sense. It is an opportunity too often overlooked. For certain, the effort must be a long-term one. Along the way, however, it is important to take advantage of the opportunity to invest in relationship skill-training.

Early in my career, I was recruited to take over the management of a nearly bankrupt company. The executive committee of the board of directors was most anxious to get someone on board to address the turnaround as soon as possible. They were extremely supportive of my recommendations on how to put the business back on solid financial footing. It involved removing two department heads who had been promoted well beyond their capabilities, restructuring the functions, and hiring three new department heads. This process took about six months, but once it was done I had a fired-up team and was able to establish a relationship with my managers that enabled the mentoring process to begin.

———— ◇ ————

A manager's technical competencies become less important, while his social skills become more important as his career progresses.

———— ◇ ————

Initially, I mentored the managers on how best to work within our overall management system. While explaining to them how *we* ran a business, I was able to show them the benefits of the various options that were available to us. But certainly the most difficult area of mentoring was dealing with the various behavior-related problems. I had not yet discovered a model such as the one presented above, which would have been quite beneficial. We'd have been better prepared to address some of the issues had such a tool been known to me at that time. We muddled through it.

I share this experience to reinforce the benefit of having in place such a convention for more readily evaluating and communicating about behavior types. What did emerge was a knowledge or awareness of varying degrees of social competence and the resultant effects on performance—and the need to develop social skills.

Social competence was something I was aware of in the context of maintaining and building relationships.

However, I was yet to learn how much it involved leadership in the various business contexts. A high level of social competence is necessary to create a level of comfort, support and enthusiasm, which are leadership skills that mentors want to cultivate. Daniel Goldman discusses the elements of interpersonal intelligence in his book, *Emotional Intelligence:*

> The argument for the importance of emotional intelligence hinges on a link between sentiment, character, and moral instincts. There is growing evidence that fundamental ethical stances in life stem from underlying emotional capacities. For one, impulse is the medium of emotion; the seed of all impulse is a feeling bursting to express itself in action. Those who are at the mercy of impulse—who lack self-control— suffer a moral deficiency: The ability to control impulse is the base of will and character. By the same token, the root of altruism lies in empathy, the ability to read emotions in others; on the other hand, if one lacks a sense of another's needs or despair, there is no caring. And if there are any two moral stances that our times call for, they are precisely these, self-restraint and compassion.

The social skills of self-restraint and compassion described by Goldman are apparent in the ability to organize groups, negotiate solutions, have empathy and create rapport. These abilities taken together represent skills that are seen as interpersonal intelligence. People who possess these skills can connect with people quite smoothly, be astute in reading the reactions and feelings, lead and organize, and handle the disputes that are bound to flare up in any human activity.

———— ◇ ————

A high level of social competence is necessary to create a level of comfort, support and enthusiasm.

———— ◇ ————

These are the natural leaders, the people who can express unspoken collective sentiment and articulate it in such a way as to lead a group toward its goals. I've most often heard the comment made about this type of person: "It is a pleasure to be around someone like that." These interpersonal abilities are just one aspect of emotional intelligence. There are numerous other manifestations, but at the heart of it is a social competency that supports the manager's leadership. Being able to understand and identify these characteristics, or lack of them, greatly enhances the mentor's ability to more comprehensively assess mentoring strategies and direction.

The following anecdote about two businesses in two different countries involves the same type of job in marketing. In the U.K. the position was called director of marketing; in the U.S. it was called vice-president.

One of my first exercises when assuming the responsibility of managing a company is to assess followership. This helps me understand who the natural leaders are, the processes they use and the results they get. Well, in the U.S. I kept hearing about this guy, "Jack," and how arrogant and demanding he was with staff members. It didn't take long to realize Jack had a serious problem. Briefly, Jack had almost no followership nor did he have much respect. He had created relationships that worked against him, making a difficult job even more difficult.

Jack had an MBA from one of the most, if not the most, prestigious graduate schools. He had exceptional credentials. Except I noticed in his employment history that he had changed jobs a lot. But the pattern was not always progressive. We talked. I asked Jack if he was aware of his general lack of support in the organization. He said he realized he could be demanding, but his level of support would just have to be subordinated to what he considered more important—which was whatever he needed done at the moment. Jack was not accustomed to working in a team environment. In fact, most of his prior experiences had been more oriented toward "individual practitioner." I called a professional associate of mine and asked him if he could help me locate an industrial psychologist. I wanted to talk to one. I needed guidance in how to counsel Jack. Early indications were that he did not realize the seriousness of his insensitivity to his colleagues.

I received the names of three industrial psychologists. I spoke to two of them and made an appointment with the one who seemed most qualified in this particular matter. After we had met twice to consider the background and issues of this particular case, I asked Jack if he would meet with the psychologist and myself to consider the situation—how I had described our problem and the psychologist's initial reaction. To Jack's credit, he said he would. The three of us met and Jack agreed to subsequent meetings with the psychologist. In fact, there were three subsequent meetings between Jack and the psychologist.

One afternoon I received a call from the psychologist. He said he had reached some conclusions regarding our matter and wondered if we could discuss it. We met. Jack had concluded that there was no reason for him to change. He just was not convinced that he was doing anything unproductive. The psychologist advised me not to expect any discernible change. The situation, in his opinion, represented a high "no-change" probability. That was not acceptable. Jack and I met and discussed our differences in perspective and the fact that, in my opinion, change was not optional. We came to an agreement. Jack would change jobs. We reached an amicable settlement and Jack departed. The best result in this situation did occur. Jack, had he been allowed to stay, would either have been miserable, trying to be someone he really wasn't, or he would have continued to demonstrate unacceptable behavior, contrary to the cultural standards. I went the extra mile with Jack because, at his age (late forties), he didn't need another career change. Also, I had inherited Jack in the organization when I was recruited. Nevertheless, the needs of the organization just could not accommodate his style. So it was resolved. That was my responsibility; to the business and my colleagues. No amount of mentoring or coaching would have been fruitful.

Nigel, whom I worked with in a U.K. company, is a different story. He wasn't yet in the position of director of marketing—he was working in an office 120 miles from headquarters in a public relations capacity. Seldom have I found anyone who had developed more followership—and he was really good at the public relations role. He also had tremendous developmental potential. Eventually, Nigel became the group director of marketing and performed with great success. He just had a charismatic ability to get people to want to help make him successful. In addition, he was a bright chap who brought keen insight to the whole marketing function. And he soaked up mentoring and coaching. I could make an observation or suggestion for consideration aimed at some particular aspect of his development. He could turn it into a positive action almost immediately, often better than I had visualized. A delightful and rewarding success story.

The issue here is to identify those who possess the social skills essential to building relationships and those who don't. If you don't have these social skills, it's extremely difficult to achieve a very impressive level of business leadership. Research has shown that most relationship skills can be improved. As you examine the learning and leadership mentoring material, performance will be enhanced by and through a comprehensive development program. The third element of the Strategic Model, relationship skills, is needed to round out the strategic mentoring focus. Just as with the other two mentoring elements, your strategy should be to build relationship skills throughout the organization, at all levels.

MENTORING RELATIONSHIP SKILLS

As developed in Chapter Four, mentoring an organization most effectively occurs at three levels—the individual, the group/team and the organization/culture. Mentoring relationship skills conforms to the same pattern. The Strategic Mentoring Model identifies the following approach in mentoring relationship skills.

Creating an awareness and appreciation individually for the importance of positive relationship skills is a crucial beginning point. This is part culture, part learning, part leadership, part team development—actually it is pervasive in the development of a high performance organization. Look at world class sports teams, or businesses that are creating world class results. There are exceptions, no doubt. But let's consider the strategies that work most of the time, not the flukes. In exceptional performance situations, arguably you will find exceptionally high levels of commitment among the participants. It is this kind of commitment that mentors want to examine to see if the same kind of relationships, which not only support superior performance but actually fuel it, can be replicated.

RELATIONSHIP-BUILDING STRATEGY

Individual	Group / Team	Organization
Facilitate developing individual relationship-building skills	Facilitate developing team relationship-building skills	Facilitate a culture that emphasizes positive working relationships
People create results, and people who work together accomplish even better results. Business usually requires people to work together for results. Therefore, effective people skills are an essential element of today's top business performers.	Groups that work well together have greater opportunity for achieving good results. Group success depends on building member relationships and drawing upon the abilities of all members.	People who work together effectively create better results. Working together effectively requires positive, supportive relationships. The organization's culture establishes the moral and ethical guidelines that create the character of the organization. The successful organization will manifest a culture built on character principles that produce excellence at all levels.

TABLE 11-4

In the process of building an organization, the logical place to strengthen the impact of effective social skills is at point of intake. Make sure the recruitment and selection process is effective in examining for this attribute. No system is foolproof but there are several good screening processes available to assist in identifying potential deficiencies—as well as strengths—in social skills. This is an area to be addressed by the human resources department. Building competence in evaluating social skills produces excellent return-on-investment.

FOUR BASIC SKILLS

One of senior management's significant responsibilities is to define the corporate vision and culture, then model and mentor it into fruition. Creating a culture that nourishes the strongest and most effective work relationships requires strategic human resource development. To achieve this end involves the development of strong relationship skills. Four specific skills emerge as major components of interpersonal or emotional intelligence. They are:

◇ *Organization*—Involves initiating and coordinating the efforts of an association of people. It is the essential skill of the leader to direct the efforts of others to achieve predetermined objectives.

◇ *Negotiation*—Involves preventing conflicts or resolving them when they do occur; demonstrated in the talent of the mediator. People who have this ability excel in finding the common thread that will create the greatest amount of support for a particular objective or solution. This is demonstrated in diplomacy or arbitration or finding the all-important middle ground that the group can support.

◇ *Empathy*—Connecting emotionally with other people. This facilitates getting involved in an encounter or recognizing and responding appropriately to people's feelings and concerns. Empathy is the art of relationship-building that supports team performance and builds *esprit de corps.*

◇ *Rapport*—Involves insightfulness regarding people's feelings, motives and concerns. Sensitivity to others' feelings leads to caring relationships, a valuable trait in building followership.

Taken together, these skills represent what is seen as interpersonal intelligence. Let's take a look these skills at the three human resource levels—those of the individual, the team and the entire organization/culture—and how they can be mentored.

―― ◇ ――

Creating a culture that nourishes the strongest and most effective work relationships requires strategic human resource development.

―― ◇ ――

MENTORING RELATIONSHIP SKILLS TO THE INDIVIDUAL

The process of mentoring relationship skills starts with awareness. The mentor in today's organizational environment is dealing with fairly enlightened folks. Successful management people I have worked with generally understand the importance of decency and fair play in the workplace.

To effectively begin the mentoring process with individuals, it is important for those involved to understand the overall mentoring objectives, processes and how they fit in. They need to make sense out of a mentoring strategy. When making a significant change in an organization, which undoubtedly will impact the culture, communicating up front what is happening avoids a lot of confusion. Then a process needs to be provided so that the person or persons who have the facts can address the questions that inevitably arise.

Mentoring relationship skills on an individual basis begins most effectively with training, in order to build understanding and awareness. I'm convinced that a well-designed training class on relationship skills is the place to start. There is major benefit from a common experience in culture building. Going through the classes together creates community as well as common language and understanding. It's a good process to use in development anytime it can be facilitated. Once there is common understanding, it is easier to mentor the kind of behavior you want to achieve.

Mentoring relationship skills is a complex process. Work colleagues possess behavioral "programming" that creates limits for change—real or imagined. Most people have what I term a "coefficient for change." That is, they have a capacity to change within certain boundaries or limits, determined by their life experiences/beliefs (programming). Everyone is unique. The flexibility to modify behavior is directly affected by this programming. For a productive discussion of this subject, I suggest Robert Bennett's book, *Gaining Control.*

As mentors, essentially you are dealing with big picture, general behavioral issues. As CEOs and managers, you are just not trained to take on significant behavioral issues. Leave it to the professionals. In this regard, I particularly call your attention to the process I followed with Jack, the marketing vice president described on page 225, whom I referred to an industrial psychologist. The problem was way too complex for my skill package. Yet, there was a lot at stake and I wanted to pursue a course of action with the greatest likelihood for the best solution. Knowing your own limitations and how not to exceed them is important, particularly in the behavioral coaching arena. I'm comfortable in dealing with the three models described above—and not being too dogmatic about it. The models should facilitate discussion, thoughtful consideration, reflection, then more discussion, always in a nonthreatening manner. Mentors are facilitators. You open windows, hopefully, through which an occasional "Aha!" will pass. Your expertise as mentors falls more in the area of creating responses of thoughtful consideration with a broader view.

As mentors, your most significant contribution to the individual in relationship-building skills is to identify the preferred behaviors—and model them.

———— ◇ ————

If the preferred behaviors are not modeled by the CEO and senior staff, they don't become the culture.

———— ◇ ————

And if the senior management team suffers unsocial behavior knowingly, that gets communicated. It's not that difficult to figure out the counterproductive impact on the culture.

MENTORING RELATIONSHIP SKILLS TO THE TEAM

Since the current trend in the workplace is for people to work together in small groups or teams, it behooves managers to seek ways to increase the effectiveness of these work units. Building relationship skills is at the heart of enhancing group effectiveness. The group or team creates a relationship experience based on individuals who are brought together for a common cause. At the heart of effective group performance is mutual support and commitment. When this exists, there is the beginning of harmony. The presence of harmony in a group is one of the enabling processes that allows the group to become a team, which has the potential of significantly increasing the quality of output. So, understanding how to achieve harmony in a group is a valuable skill.

ALIGNMENT AND ATTUNEMENT

Energy and creativity, which support personal effectiveness, usually manifest in the workplace when the organization's purposes are clear, understood as meaningful, and generally supported. People are inclined to perform work that gives them a sense of accomplishment; usually they are having fun, or at least enjoying the work processes; and they are learning to care for the people they work with. This is *alignment*—organization members acting as part of an integrated whole—and it happens when individuals expand their individual purpose to include the organization's purpose. *Attunement* is an equally important contributor to effective group performance. Attunement is a term that originated from a musical concept, but has real and meaningful application to an organizational context. Resonance, or harmony among the parts of the system, occurs when there is alignment.

HARMONY

Alignment and attunement support the development of an integrated unity and harmony among the various parts of the system. And it is in this type of environment that exceptional performance most readily occurs.

I draw these conclusions from experiences in two separate contexts: music and business. First, music. My long-time hobby of playing the mandolin has placed me in numerous music ensembles. Where there is alignment and attunement among the musicians, the musical experience and its quality create enormous satisfaction. When absent, when there is tension or worse, the musicians struggle, the activity just isn't any fun, which is reflected in the results. And each of the players is capable of so much more!

I have seen this same phenonenon in the business environment. A group of bright, capable people, apparently working in concert, get demotivated or upset over some situation that negatively impacts the group alignment and attunement. The creative processes collapse and people go into cruise-control, fire-fighting or self-preservation.

The effective remedy for this problem is awareness, understanding and commitment—on an individual basis. This is part of the culture you are attempting to create in the strategic mentoring process: an environment in which individuals take responsibility not only for results but for conditions that can change ordinary results into exceptional results. This process starts with the commitment to create positive relationships that support harmony, focus and excellence.

MENTORING RELATIONSHIP SKILLS TO THE CULTURE

Although a lot already has been said about the importance of modeling in establishing the culture, it is important to again emphasize that no one does it more effectively than the senior management team. They are the cultural trend-setters. This applies to just about every action every day. They are always "on." Particularly when it comes to relationships.

Not too long ago, a senior level executive from a sister company to the one I was managing visited my office. We were in a meeting when his office called. My secretary passed him the note, he jumped up and walked out to her desk. He spoke to his colleague, concluded his conversation, then proceeded to tell my secretary to order him a taxi. Not so much as a please or thank you. Like many executives who have highly effective assistants as their executive secretaries, I have always treated my assistant, June, as a partner/colleague—I would bring coffee to her almost as often as she brought it to me. She would go through a wall for me; I would try to do the same for her. Well, can you imagine what an impression was made by that executive? He had just bashed a relationship and in the process had dealt this particular culture a negative blow. And it happens so often in corporate circles by folks who should know better. Hey, the fantastically committed mailperson deserves the same amount of respect as the CEO. That is, of course, if you really want a culture that supports an empowered and empowering bunch of colleagues who produce exceptional results.

Let's reconsider a term introduced in Chapter Ten—*workleader.* What you should develop in your organization, in order to truly see it empowered, are workleaders throughout the enterprise. Workleaders are the colleagues who should be involved in continuous learning, leading with that knowledge and enhanced by their social intelligence. That is your model; workleaders modeling top achievement in learning, leading and relating—individually, in teams, and throughout the organization.

———— ◇ ————

The mailperson deserves the same amount of respect as the CEO.

———— ◇ ————

The workleaders aren't just the CEO and the department heads. They exist at every level and are contributing to the total effort. Your strategy on a day-to-day basis is to maintain that kind of momentum.

MENTOR'S CHECKUP

◇ What proactive steps could be taken to tweak your culture to make it more relationship-smart?

◇ To what extent are teams or work-groups the definitive work unit in your organization? Could their effectiveness be improved? How?

◇ Of the four described behavior styles (Table 11-3), which are most prominent in your organization's senior management group? How does it affect the culture?

◇ Study the performance of one of your colleagues who is particularly skilled in establishing rapport. Is his/her followership at the expected level? Why?

PART IV

THE WAY FORWARD

CHAPTERS 12-14

CHAPTER TWELVE

DECIDING TO BE A MENTOR

OVERVIEW

Take a moment and think about the people in your life who have made significant contributions to your development. Most people can single out one or two contributors in their personal and professional lives who were standouts. They came along at a time when there was a developmental need or opportunity and they added real value. I think of the several mentors who have made that contribution on behalf of my life. The results they helped create were extra-special and certainly beyond the grasp of my own abilities at that moment. Personalized guidance and focused assistance—what resources to have available!

With that perspective, I believe any business manager who is motivated toward high achievement will want to employ the benefits of mentoring. In Chapter Four the Strategic Mentoring Model identified the three levels of mentoring. This chapter acquaints the reader with the requirements and strategies for becoming an effective mentor.

Communication skills rank high on the list of requirements for successful mentoring. The guidance process requires a sensitive exchange of information to assist those being mentored to discover expanded options. The tactful and intelligent use of questions enables the mentor to guide without directing—an important distinction for development. This chapter presents material on the methods and types of questions that evoke creative thinking.

BECOMING A MENTOR

Not every mentor is a manager; however, every manager who truly wants to be as effective as possible will want to become a mentor. Understanding how to be a mentor or introducing the opportunity to become a mentor carries with it a large, economy-size opportunity. If members of the management group, which consists of everyone bearing the title of manager, are to be effective mentors, then preparation is essential. Just deciding that you want to become a mentor is the first step. From my experiences in mentoring mentors, I have identified certain phases one goes through on the way to understanding what mentoring really is. There are, in fact, four phases that managers go through to become committed mentors:

1. AWARENESS

First, the candidate needs to become aware of what mentoring is, what mentors do, and what a mentoring program looks like and can accomplish.

2. UNDERSTANDING AND APPRECIATION

Next comes the need to understand what can be accomplished through mentoring and the candidate's particular role in the process. This should lead to an appreciation of the value of the process of mentoring, including the value both to the individual and to the business.

3. ADVOCACY

Supporting the cause is essential to becoming a participant. Since all managers have a responsibility to develop people, this simply is a matter of the potential candidate coming to grips with that responsibility and seeing mentoring as an excellent facilitator.

4. COMMITMENT

Commitment puts legs on advocacy. It's one thing to see the benefits and agree that the concept has merit, but doing it is what provides the value. Commitment to facilitating the process and becoming involved in mentoring is the final stage of resourcing the process.

A discussion of the process of implementing a company-wide mentoring program was presented in Chapter Five (Table 5-1, page 71) presents the steps in the implementation and maintenance cycle. The third and fourth steps in this cycle are Education and Understanding, and Participation and Buy-in. The four phases described above (Awareness, Understanding and Appreciation, Advocacy, Commitment) accomplish the third and fourth steps. The fifth step in the implementation cycle is management and leadership involvement in the actual mentoring—to become mentors. Most members of senior management staffs find mentoring to be rewarding at a very high level. ·

THE CREDIBILITY ISSUE

An individual's character, one's trustworthiness, is at the heart of mentorship. The credibility that allows you to be a mentor must be supported by character and competence. Consider the competence issue for a moment. What do leaders who qualify as mentors do to remain in that position? First, they are continually learning. They are constantly taking new information on board. They read, they seek training, they listen, they learn from whatever sources they can. They constantly expand their competence. They develop new skills, new interests and discover that the more they know, the more they realize what they need to know. Most of this learning and growth energy is self-initiated and self-perpetuating.

CHARACTERISTICS OF AN EFFECTIVE MENTOR

At the heart of successful mentoring is relationship. Second, the credentials of the mentor must provide evidence of his ability to lead a growth process on behalf of the people being mentored, enabling them to accept his leadership. While the mentor does not need to have the specific answers for which the mentee may be looking, he should be skilled in *directing* the search for answers in a constructive manner. Also, he should be able to communicate in such a way as to validate the content and create enthusiasm in the recipient. For this to happen the mentee must ascribe to the mentor the role of contributor and counselor. The mentee will recognize that the mentor has something to contribute that will enhance his overall performance and success.

How does this happen? Over the years I've seen numerous situations where mentoring was taking place and I can only describe what I believe to be the major contributors. At the core of it is the skill and personality of the mentor. There is a sense of caring and empathy that contribute to the mentee's success. Further, the mentee seems to understand and validate the process. It seems very "old worldly" in the sense of the relationship between master/apprentice or teacher/student.

For the most effective results to occur the mentor and mentee enter a growth partnership. To do this demands a great deal of credibility on the part of the mentor. True mentoring will only occur if the mentee can see the value in the process. This translates to accepting that the mentor really can provide meaningful direction to growth and development. The mentor must possess something that at the moment the mentee doesn't have but desires. To do this, he must be convinced that the mentor, first and foremost cares. Knowledge isn't always the commodity being given. Frequently, it's creative direction, confirmation or enhancement. The process creates an opportunity for what I call "synergistic collaboration." In my experience, many an "Aha!" has come from these encounters.

So, the particular qualities in mentors that seem to contribute to their effectiveness are these:

1. SOCIAL SKILLS

Frankly, not every manager I've met seems to be endowed with vast quantities of this wonderful commodity—social skills and/or emotional intelligence. I've seen a number of chief executives who had not necessarily achieved their position based on outstanding people-handling skills. Further, the thought of mentoring probably hadn't even occurred to many of them. For someone to be an effective mentor, they must first see value in the process. Then, there must be an understanding of what is involved to achieve success as a mentor. There must be desire as well as credibility to pull it off. This is not an easy task. Just because one has senior manager or executive status does not mean he is going to be accepted as one of his colleagues' mentors. Such status can only be granted by the potential mentee.

You are all aware that one does not have to be exceptional at handling people to be a successful manager. There are other attributes that are very important in achieving business objectives. But I still believe that even a very effective manager, who has driven his organization to achieve exceptional results, could and should play a role in the mentoring process. He is in a position to provide valuable guidance.

2. INTEGRITY

Another crucial attribute for a mentor is integrity. The person must be viewed by colleagues as someone who is fair-minded, ethical and willing to treat people with dignity and respect. Before you can confer with someone and provide counsel, he has to be in a position to want it or he won't take it. Integrity precedes trust, which creates the foundation for any relationship.

3. TRUST

Trust must be at the top of the list of a mentor's essential characteristics. And the concept must work in both directions—the mentor must be trusted by the mentee and in turn the mentor must trust the mentee. Mentoring relationships requires mutual trust as the foundation for the intense, in-depth, inherently sensitive issues that emerge in the process. Each person needs to make sure that confidences are not betrayed. Meaningful communication and problem resolution can only occur if the trust factor is not in question.

4. RESPECT

Closely connected to trust is respect. Just as with trust, respect must be mutually held. Respect is required if you are to have a successful relationship that enables the mentee to experience growth and development. Respect not only is associated with the relationship between individuals but also in terms of respective frames of reference or patterns of belief. Respect for someone's background and traditions may well enter into the communication process as the mentoring process develops. Respect for experiences in situations that both parties have gone through to develop their frames of reference is an important developmental ingredient. Opinions may differ but respect for those opinions and views should be constant.

5. KNOWLEDGE

A major contributor to a mentor's credibility and influence is knowledge. What does he have to offer? If the mentor has not been addressing his own personal growth by acquiring new information and enhancing his own abilities, then it's going to be a difficult task for him to contribute to others' growth. It is my observation that the managers who have been committed to continuous learning have knowledge and experience to share that will have meaning for their colleagues. Now, in many organizations the weeding out process would provide us with managers who are committed to growth. I know that's what I was seeking when I've promoted managers into executive slots. To lead his organization to success and to develop stronger managers who will become the executives of the future, an executive must be in a state of growth. If an executive has committed himself to continuous learning and growth, then he is likely to be a good candidate either to mentor or to become a mentor. In that case he possesses what his colleagues need— knowledge and the understanding of how to use it in a particular context.

6. PERSPECTIVE AND PARTNERING

Mentors need to be able to see the big picture and fit the pieces together to create harmony, support and direction. Helping those being mentored to see how they fit into the scheme of things, to understand their contribution to it and to plan their career direction is of great value. Also, interacting in a partner mode, based on a sense of "We're all in this together" establishes the relationship and communication on a much deeper and more meaningful level. It is in this state that the mentor can best demonstrate that he cares.

7. PASSION

Have you ever noticed how some people are constantly cheerful, pleasant or upbeat? Their spirit is enthusiastic and hopeful. This kind of positive energy provides a kind of energy field that surrounds the person and imbues him with a certain pleasant and approachable countenance that is attractive to people. These people enchant everyone they meet.

A person who really cares deeply for something he is involved in exudes passion and is exciting to be around. He just seems to generate enthusiasm. This characteristic adds dramatically to a mentor's impact on what he does and says. Several years ago I enjoyed working with a wonderful manager from the U.K., Andrew Quicke, who just exuded excitement for life itself. His enthusiasm was demonstrated for the project he was working on, the meeting he was in, or whatever he was doing. Andrew attracted people to his cause because he always seemed to be thoroughly enjoying whatever he was doing. He really mentored me in understanding the power of passion, even in the little things. Andrew is still my model and mentor for genuine enthusiasm and passion. He knows how to light up a roomful of people.

8. CONFIDENCE IN PEOPLE

I worked with an entrepreneur for a while who seemed to take delight in snatching dignity from others. Whenever he noticed a less-than-stellar performance by someone else, he seemed compelled to bring it to the attention of the person with whom he was dealing. The harm was in the manner in which he did it. Usually, it was in a not-so-pleasant manner. It was called in that particular environment "getting zapped." Unfortunately, as an entrepreneur, he had built a business that relied almost entirely on his personal knowledge and decision-making abilities. As a result, he had produced a cadre of undertrained managers. As these managers began to develop increased knowledge about preferred management practices, they realized that they had been subjected to bad management practices. This was not an energized or motivated group of managers, and the overall leadership and management performance showed it.

Those who can contribute to growth in others are able to convey their confidence and belief in others. In that regard, you must strive to believe in unseen potential, which creates a climate for growth and development. Self-confident people often believe that the solutions lie within themselves and in their particular strategies. This same self-confidence can be useful for cultivating creativity in others and urging them to manifest it productively. The result is that an extremely valuable asset, an enthusiastic team of workleaders, is unleashed.

9. BALANCE

So many executives fall into the trap of becoming narrow in their outlook and approach to life. It is easy to be so consumed by one's business interests that the perspective on other issues is lost. Attainment of balance is essential. Balanced executives with balanced lives read good literature and magazines and keep up with current events. They are actively interested in music, sports, theater or other interests that are rejuvenating. Also, such a balance contributes to a more relaxed lifestyle that includes having fun, maintaining a sense of humor and the ability to laugh at themselves. They are honest with themselves. Their actions and attitudes are appropriate, temperate and wise. Balance enables them to come to the job on Monday mornings with the enthusiasm necessary to create an environment in which people can attain excellence.

MENTORING/MANAGING

According to arguments advanced by some management writers, managers have a responsibility to mentor those whom they manage. No disagreement here. A good manager should be a good coach, providing regular feedback, encouragement and help to his staff member to enhance development and growth. Who better than a person's manager can provide enlightened development guidance? And yet, while it sounds great, in reality I just haven't found enough of it in the workplace to indicate that it happens with any predictability.

—— ◇ ——

A serious problem inherent in the whole area of management development is that too many managers are given the management title without the management training.

—— ◇ ——

The various organizations in which I have assumed management or advisory responsibility had a nearly uniform practice of promoting people to management positions without providing fundamental training to prepare them for such roles, and I don't think those organizations are unique. When coming into an organization, my focus has been to address management development deficiencies. I have high expectations of my management colleagues. My expectations have sometimes exceeded their understanding and preparation to respond to those expectations. Thus, I have often had to lead a growth process. It is an important process that ensures fundamental management principles are held in common and that the team understands the processes that the CEO expects to find in use within the business. I have found great value in mentoring my managers *en group.*

While the human-resource development process should address the basic factors involved in being a manager, it also provides an opportunity to extend the development process to include learning, leading and relationship-building. Getting managers involved in this process contributes to making it part of the culture—it takes it out of the personnel department and transforms it into "on-the-job training."

MENTOR DEVELOPMENT

Just as there is a need for managers to be trained in effective management, the same holds true for mentors. Many large organizations in the United States and the United Kingdom have found value in creating internal mentor training programs. Some programs provide mentors to new employees to help them through their early indoctrination into the corporate culture. On a more sophisticated level, some companies have a mentoring program in which promising young "stars" are identified and put on the fast track. By fast-tracking, the individual is assigned a mentor to guide his overall management development in order to accelerate his placement on the senior management team. These types of programs vary with the size and type of business. The key point is that a successful mentoring program requires trained mentors.

GETTING STARTED

Certainly, one can become a mentor in an organization without the existence of a formal mentoring program. These types of relationships sprout in many organizations based on need and opportunity. After having noticed the value of formalizing such a program, however, some CEOs have made this an important part of the corporate development strategy.

A mentoring program is most successful when it helps a corporation set the stage to become a more effective player in the business environment. Having front-ended the process with a perpetuation plan for the business and the executive team, meaningful direction also is provided for the whole mentoring process. Subsequently, the mentoring program will consistently support the strategic development efforts of the company. After that, it's a matter of selecting and training mentors to support this strategic objective. This can really create some pretty exciting dynamics among the company's most important resources. I can think of no better investment than getting top management turned on and excited about strategic people development in order to perpetuate the business.

———— ◇ ————

Imagine an environment where every executive
has his own personal-growth coach.

———— ◇ ————

Hey, I'm a believer. If I could achieve it, I would have every member of my senior management group working with a mentor. I would want to make sure that they are qualified mentors and that we achieve the very best results from the process. We are talking about creating some pretty impressive results!

FIRST PERSON THOUGHTS ON THE MENTORING EXPERIENCE

Now that I'm a mentor, I realize this is a big responsibility and I want to get it right. I'm about to enter into a relationship with a mentee in which I want to create value. This is a significant responsibility, since I realize I will be serving as a *guide* to this individual's future success. For the process to really work, I need to have all of my creative juices flowing. I need to get into my best "game mind-set."

First, I want to make sure that when I meet with my mentee I understand the mission. Right up front I want to make sure he has a good understanding of short-term, mid-term, and long-term objectives. So, we're going to sit down and go through his agenda to make sure I understand where he's coming from. What is it I can help him do? In that respect I want to make sure that I've got my listening skills up to snuff. I want to make sure my receptors are open. I want to talk for a while with this mentee and find out what he is about, where he is coming from, where he hurts, what makes him laugh, what makes him feel good or bad. In this initial meeting I will do the groundbreaking work of establishing the relationship. My initial responsibility is to establish that relationship. It is the conduit through which all the rest of the meaningful processes will be channeled.

MENTOR/MENTEE RAPPORT

How can I, in as short a time as possible, help establish an effective relationship? First, my mentee has to know that I'm approachable and that I care. I want to create a setting where the mentee feels absolutely comfortable in opening up and sharing any particular issues that he wants to address in terms of increasing his effectiveness and growing his career. So, initially, what you need to do is establish rapport. Mentoring works best when it is mentee-driven.

Throughout this process there will be tremendous pressure on the mentor to maintain rapport. By this I mean the need to be totally honest, doing it in a way that doesn't put the focus on the individual, but rather on the process and the subject matter. Foremost in the mentor's mind is the need to be a candid guide throughout the process. As a mentor, I am facilitating a process that will enable the mentee to expand his understanding and achieve optimum direction and outcome in his developmental trip.

INTERACTIVE COMMUNICATION

One of the more effective ways to guide the mentoring process is through questioning and listening. The mentor should not prescribe, but, instead should be the catalyst that enables the mentee to "open another window" into the realm of solutions. Questions feed the process. They need to be *open-ended questions.* Such questions generally are used to draw out a wide range of responses on a broad topic. These questions come in many forms and frequently are used by interactive managers. Open questions usually:

◇ Cannot be answered by a simple Yes or No.

◇ Begin with What, How or Why.

◇ Do not lead the mentee in a specific direction.

◇ Increase dialogue by drawing out the mentee's feelings and opinions.

◇ Can be used to encourage your mentee to elaborate on objectives, needs, wants, problems and current situations.

◇ Help the mentee to discover things for himself

◇ Can be used to stimulate the mentee to think about your ideas

◇ Allow your mentee to exhibit his "style" much more readily and accurately than any other type of question

Some examples of open questions are:

◇ How do you feel about your present job performance?

◇ What are the ways you feel this should be handled?

◇ Why do you feel this has been happening so frequently and for so long?

◇ What do you think about it?

◇ What other objectives do you think you should be pursuing at this time?

◇ What do you feel is most important right now in terms of your present job responsibilities?

◇ What do you like least about your present situation?

◇ Who else is involved in that problem?

◇ How important is that solution to you?

◇ What do you think would happen if you implemented this solution?

◇ What are the implications if this situation continues?

◇ What are the behaviors you want to see?

◇ What are outcomes and how will you know they have been achieved?

FEELING/FINDING QUESTIONS

This type of question usually is manifested in the form of an open-ended question. These questions are used to probe deeper into the mentee's thinking, attitudes, convictions, motivations and feelings. This often can be a sensitive situation for the mentee. Thus, it is important to keep in mind that a strong rapport and bond of trust must be established before pursuing some of these types of questions. The objective is to help the mentee develop a better understanding of how certain behaviors are created. Significant personal insight can be brought to the mentee as a result of asking him these types of questions. Used properly, they allow the mentee to dig deeper into his thinking about why he feels or behaves the way he does. They help the individual discover for himself what drives him. He is allowed to discover problems for himself and internal motivations for his behavior. With this added insight, he is much more willing to question some of the principles that drive his behavior.

Feeling/finding questions usually take the following forms:

◇   How did you come to feel this way about your job?

◇   To what extent do you feel your personal and professional goals and objectives are being met by your present job classification?

◇   Why do you feel that this is the best approach?

◇   What do you feel are the least effective/most effective ways of accomplishing this particular job?

◇   How do you feel this situation came about?

◇   What do you like least/most about the way this problem has been handled to date?

◇   What is your opinion?

◇   How many other people do you feel are in a similar situation?

◇   What is your opinion on how this can best be handled?

◇   How do you feel the problem should be approached?

DEVELOPMENTAL QUESTIONS

This type of question is designed to draw out a broad response on a topic. They can help you:

◇ Ask for additional information in a more detailed format

◇ Encourage the employee to expand and or elaborate upon a topic that already has been introduced. Some examples are:

* Can you give me an example of what you mean by that?

* Then what?

* Would you please elaborate on that point?

* Can you tell me more about it?

* Do you recall what other types of problems you were confronted with in that situation?

* What other things do you like to do in your spare time?

THIRD PARTY QUESTIONS

This particular type of question combines a statement and a question. This is a terrific tool to use to introduce a concept; for example, using a Peter Drucker quote and then getting a reaction to it. Research indicates that there is greater acceptance of a statement if it is attributed to a respected person or institution. Therefore, you may be enhancing your position by mentioning the names of recognized leaders in that field who support your position. Specific third-party questions take the following form:

◇ Peter Drucker believes that the hiring of managers who lack integrity is a reflection on the character of the leadership of the company. How do you feel about that?

◇ John Brown, our vice president of finance, feels that you should lower your costs and, at the same time, increase your revenues by dropping your losing product lines. What's your opinion?

Okay, those were specific, now let's look at general third-party questions and see what you can do with these:

◇ Most management people I talk to tell me this is the case. Do you find this to be true?

⬦ Many of my colleagues tell me that this is the most rewarding aspect of the job. What is your opinion?

⬦ A lot of managers I talk to feel that proactive, daily time management is important. How do you feel about that?

TESTING QUESTIONS

These are questions aimed at determining the state of mind or present position of an individual on a specific issue. They are useful when you need to determine your mentee's limit of agreement or disagreement on specific factors or points that have been brought up during the conversation. Testing questions take the following form:

⬦ How does that come across to you?

⬦ How important is that to you?

⬦ Does that make sense to you?

⬦ How agreeable are you on that issue?

⬦ Do you think you can live with that?

CLOSURE QUESTIONS

These are good questions to encourage agreement and promote successful implementation of a suggested plan or solution. Closure questions usually are open-ended, but with direction. For example, "Where do you go from here?" is a well-used closure question. It's open but it directs the mentee to commit to a particular direction. Either way, the mentee is asked to make a commitment. Other closure questions include:

⬦ How would you like to proceed with this?

⬦ What action would you like to take?

⬦ What do you see is the next step in the decision process?

⬦ How should you come to closure on this situation?

⬦ What's the next move?

By skillfully administering questions, the mentor may probe and stimulate the thinking of the mentee to move him away from a particular position that may be blocking him. Or, if nothing else, such questions will help the mentee gain clarity on his sense of himself, where he is going and what he hopes to accomplish. The communication process enables the mentor and mentee to develop a clear understanding of the direction the mentoring process will take.

MENTORING AND COMMUNICATION

Mentoring relationships may be developed at several levels of effectiveness. The levels are dependent on the quality and types of relationships. Mentoring is relationship-driven. The level at which the relationship has developed will determine the effectiveness of the mentoring. In Chapter Eleven, the four basic relationship skills were discussed (Organization, Negotiation, Empathy and Rapport). The latter two, empathy and rapport, seem to have the greatest impact on the quality of communication, the relationship, and, subsequently, the mentoring.

In the context of relationships, consider the three targets for mentoring presented in the Strategic Model. Developing a relationship with the organization requires a different strategy from, say, developing a relationship with the individual. Mentoring the organization and the group is better accomplished through leadership and modeling. Having said that, the ability to communicate and relate to people greatly facilitates the mentoring process at all three levels. The impact of the mentor is influenced heavily by the level of communication achieved. For your purposes, I will identify four levels of communication:

Four Communication Levels

I.   *Formal*–Usually manifested in large groups, regarding such matters as diplomacy, official government social affairs or high-level church meetings. Social distance is maintained and little personal information is shared among the group members. Rarely would a mentor get personal under these circumstances.

II. *Informal*–Found in small group environments where most people are acquainted on a first-name basis and share common experiences. They may share personal feelings on occasion.

III. *Familial*–This level normally would be found among long-time family friends, old school chums, people who have grown up together–close relationships. They usually share sincere feelings, with some reservations in some instances.

IV. *Intimate*–Usually exists between family members, husband and wife, life-long friends and the like. Generally, members share intimate feelings.

In this model, the most effective level of communication, in terms of relationship development, occurs at Level IV-Intimate. To achieve meaningful mentoring, level III-Familial, would support an effective mentoring relationship, particularly at a one-on-one level. It would be difficult for me to imagine a very productive mentoring relationship developing at Level I; Level II would work, but perhaps the greatest benefit could be developed in a Level III setting.

I have encountered a few managers, very few thank goodness, who never seemed to get beyond Level I in their communication development. In a conversation it's almost like an invisible barrier is placed between us. I can understand this happening with strangers, but not with people you work with for months and months, even years. The person I described in Chapter Eleven as "Jack" had this problem, among others. And he had little positive effect on anyone. Conclusion? To be an effective mentor, take a look at your communication and relationship-building skills. What can you improve? If you're unsure, ask your mentor.

THE MENTOR AS LISTENER

Asking thought-provoking questions makes a serious contribution to the guidance process. However, without sensitive listening, the full potential is not reached. In fact, this is where one-on-one mentoring begins. To be effective, the mentor has to listen even to the unspoken message. Being a good listener is the first step in approachability, which in turn nurtures a deeper level of communication.

With virtually tons of written material available on the importance of listening, I'm generally dismayed at the competence level of management-listening skills. I made it a project recently to proactively assess the "listening profile" of the managers I have been working with and around. Perhaps because of the competition to be heard, to be recognized or to get on to the next agenda item, there is an apparent epidemic of poor listening habits. Many people seem to only be marking time when another party is speaking, just waiting for the next opportunity to jump in. All the while they were engrossed in preparing their next remarks, rather than really listening to the other person. If you have been on the receiving end of this type of communication, there is a temptation to call a time-out and review the ground rules of effective communication.

—— ◇ ——

The mentor has to listen even to
the unspoken message.

—— ◇ ——

It's important to call attention to this problem in the mentoring context in order to underscore the importance of listening when the objective is to build rapport. Essentially, it is one of the key social skills employed in establishing relationships. For the mentor, listening becomes an art. Effective mentors don't listen passively. They listen dramatically, often restating the mentee's comments to assure clarity. When people feel they've really been heard, they feel valued. Feeling valued enhances the quality of the relationship, enabling even more meaningful communication to occur. There are a lot of mentoring opportunities in the field of listening. Certainly, listening-preparedness should be the first skill evaluated before a potential mentor is allowed to take on such a sensitive role.

DEVELOPING AS A MENTOR

The job is never finished. As humans, we always represent personal-development potential, another good lesson to be learned, or a new fact to add to the data bank. Learning is never completed, so development continues as long as you can draw a breath. In fact, studies confirm that it is a significant life-lengthening activity. Since everything is either in growth or decay, I want to support as much growth in my own life as I possibly can. As I age, the forces of decay continually threaten the balance. So I'll take more growth anytime! Aside from fostering longevity, remaining in a growth-mode also makes me a better mentor.

MENTOR'S CHECKUP

◊ What results do you think could be improved in your organization through mentoring?

◊ What skills would you want to hone to improve your mentoring capabilities? Do you have a mentor to help make that happen?

◊ How would you describe your organization's commitment to learning? How would you describe yours?

◊ How do you rate yourself as a listener? How do you think your colleagues would rate you? Why not ask a couple of them?

CHAPTER THIRTEEN

DECIDING TO BE A MENTEE

OVERVIEW

The mentor-mentee relationship creates an excellent partnership opportunity for personal growth. This chapter focuses on what the mentee can do to increase the quality of the results. The importance of self-direction and discipline are developed as part of the mentee's contribution to the mentoring process.

No doubt many of you have looked back at your careers and wondered how you got where you did and what you could have done differently. Particularly if the results were more attributable to circumstances than design. In a rapidly changing business environment, more careers are being impacted by circumstances—such as downsizing, mergers and acquisitions—than ever before. More than ever, strategic career planning can be an effective countermeasure against some "unavoidable" negative events. As the old adage goes, the best defense is a good offense. That is particularly true in career management. And one of the best ways to guide career development is with the help of an effective mentor. And what does an effective mentor want? An effective mentee! Let's consider now what a mentee can contribute to the mentoring process to attain the best results.

THE BIG PICTURE

There are two ways to approach this subject. You can look at being an effective mentee from the point-of-view of an organization that is establishing a mentoring program and, as a result, is looking for the most effective mentees. Or you can look at the issue with the view that, ideally, you should all be mentees and, in that case, ask how then should you approach your own development. That's the approach I will be taking, which is supported by the strong belief that each of us is responsible for his own growth and development. As such, being a mentee is one more avenue of approach to achieving continuous growth. Let's examine how this can be accomplished.

Business literature is full of admonitions regarding the importance of taking personal responsibility for your own growth. At this point I shall not review that literature other than to underscore the importance of a self-directed development program. Who better knows the proper direction for development to take than the mentee? There are various names that are used in business literature for the person involved in the learning journey, including mentee, protege, learner, student and intern, to name only some of the more popular ones. For our purposes, I will continue to use the term mentee.

I firmly believe that all who are interested in developing their careers in order to achieve their potential should be involved in a mentoring program. Yes, everyone needs a mentor. I speak with some conviction since, as a mentee, I've personally experienced the benefits from this process. So, I'm communicating to you on the basis of first-hand experience that it has extremely high value when it works properly. And that's what you want to examine; how can you, as mentees, bring as much to the process to make it as effective as possible?

WHAT DO YOU WANT?

You have all been thrown into the deep end of this process we call life. What you get out of it has much to do with choices you make along the way. Your life is or will be the total of all the choices you make, both unconsciously and consciously. The same is true of your careers. Eventually you get to the point in your professional life where you start to wind down. It is at that point that you feel pride or regret over your career and the choices you made. Had you been mentored throughout your career, your choices might have resulted in fewer mistakes and more successes.

—— ◇ ——

For most people, circumstances rather than choices determine the courses of their careers.

—— ◇ ——

If the mentee can receive direction in this process of choice-making, he should be able to take some control over the direction of his career. This is an interesting phenomenon—control. Taking control of your life, taking control of your career.

Only infrequently do people actually achieve what they long for in their careers. And when they do achieve their objectives, it is usually the result of a series of thoughtful choices. For most people, however, circumstances rather than choices determine the courses of their careers. On the other hand, I've noticed that people who have achieved fulfillment in their careers are those who are in control—of themselves, their careers and the relationships and conditions around them. Now, by control I'm not talking about some heavy-handed or clandestine, manipulative process. Rather, being in control means having an awareness of choices and being proactive in their pursuit. I merely want to point out the importance of realizing the need to make choices rather than acquiescing to circumstances. At the heart of the choice process, however, is the matter of identifying what it is you really want.

CLARIFYING QUESTIONS

◇ What do you want out of life?

◇ Where do you want to be one year from now?

◇ Where do you want to be three to five years from now?

◇ Can these objectives be attained within your current organization?

◇ What kind of sacrifices are you willing to make to achieve these objectives?

◇ Do you really understand why you are trying to achieve these objectives, and are they consistent with your philosophy of life?

◇ Are there any inconsistencies between your objectives and your current behaviors?

An earnest and thoughtful evaluation will ultimately lead to the question, "What do I need to do to achieve these objectives?"

BEING ALL YOU CAN BE

To start the process, you need to consciously acknowledge that you are taking responsibility for your own growth and development. Something that keeps coming to mind is the admonition of an old colleague of mine. There are so many applications for it, I just keep using it: *You either take what you get, or you get what you plan.* At the heart of this aphorism is the concept of initiative. And that's where the mentoring process has to start. Responsibility and initiative are the foundational principles upon which you start to build your own growth and development.

———— ◇ ————

The road to success is to realize your potential and act on it.

———— ◇ ————

A few years back the U.S. Army's recruiting slogan said, "Be all you can be." I like that. This type of thinking was common in the character/ethic literature of the 19th and early 20th centuries—the Benjamin Franklin philosophy. It seems to emphasize that there are no shortcuts. There's a price to pay for achieving success. It can't be made to look too easy because it really isn't. Success is the result of a focused, diligent effort to achieve predetermined objectives. The road to success is to realize your potential and to act on it.

DEVELOPMENT DRIVEN BY CHARACTER VERSUS PERSONALITY

In the past twenty years there has been enormous emphasis on self-development and self-improvement. Literally dozens of speakers on the business-seminar circuit specialize in self-improvement training. While there's a place for this type of training in your development programs, my concern is that usually it focuses on the wrong issues. Taking responsibility for your own development requires the ability to, in effect, change yourself. That is, to create self-initiated change within your performance package. You change yourself through the growth process. And change at a meaningful level usually is the result of a very thoughtful process that involves reassessment of some of your basic principles. It's not a quick-fix process. Frequently, business seminars that stress personal change stimulate only "pep rally" excitement that fizzles before the participants arrive home. To create true developmental change, it is necessary to endure the pain of going back and looking at principles of behavior that are rooted in your character.

Success literature has been a vital segment of American business literature for some time. In fact, it goes back some 200 years. In the first 150 years it focused on character. But the past fifty years have focused more on personality. And success literature of the past fifty years is superficial compared with some of the older literature. The earlier material, based on character ethics, placed the foundation for success in characteristics such as integrity, humility, fidelity, temperance, courage, justice, patience, industry, simplicity, modesty, and the Golden Rule. Benjamin Franklin's autobiography stands out as an excellent example of this type of literature.

The character ethic emphasized that basic principles, when applied, help produce effective living. And people can only experience true success if these principles are integrated into their basic character. However, there seemed to be a shift from the *character ethic* to the *personality ethic* shortly after World War I.

The recent approach to success, based more on personality factors, such as public image, attitudes and behaviors, are skills and techniques that enhance human-interaction processes. The personality ethic is manifested in two different ways. First, through human and public relations techniques and, second, through positive mental attitude. Elements of this approach seem to be more manipulative, even bordering on deception. It encourages people to use these techniques to get other people to do what they want and, in effect, to "use" them.

I believe it is important to make the distinction between the two approaches—character versus personality—in order to identify what I believe to be a more legitimate and longer-lasting form of development.

It is not my purpose to say that personality-based development is not valid or legitimate. Training, such as public speaking, developing confidence in making presentations and the like, certainly have application. Even the positive-thinking programs have their place. But as students of behavioral change, it is important that you differentiate among them to understand where the enduring types of development should be based. That comes back to character.

———— ◇ ————

The people who attain the higher levels of responsibility are usually the ones who have had the discipline to develop the necessary skills

———— ◇ ————

An understanding of Covey's material (from his book *The 7 Habits of Highly Effective People*) regarding the first three habits, which he calls the "private victory," provide an excellent framework for looking at self-development. I have encountered numerous colleagues on the road to self-development. There are some dropouts, unfortunately, who didn't and don't achieve what they set out to achieve. I've attempted to examine what it takes for people to create the kind of change they say they want.

My assessment is that the one major necessary ingredient is *discipline*. It is interesting that some hopeful management students, who wish to advance their careers, lack the self-discipline to develop the necessary skills, abilities and understanding to achieve what they say they want. I have encountered a number of folks who say they want to accomplish something, but never quite seem to have the willpower or the self-discipline to do it. Certainly the question has been raised in management literature that if one is incapable of managing one's self, is he then really qualified to manage others? No doubt there are exceptions to that apparently obvious answer, but on the whole it is probably fairly representative of "real world" truths. The people who attain the higher levels of responsibility are usually the ones who have had the discipline to develop the necessary skills and abilities to handle increased responsibilities. And the process was usually a rigorous one, requiring discipline.

THE RIGHT DIRECTION— MANAGEMENT

There is a huge opportunity in the business environment to help produce clarity about the real world of professional management early in a manager's career. I appreciate the efforts that our esteemed and learned colleagues at the universities are making. However, there seems to be an opportunity and a need for a practicum in "What It Is Really Like." I'm sure this need exists in all the professions. There seems to be a need to bridge the gap between leaving the learned institutional halls and being involved in the day-to-day management environment. The same could be said about other professions— law, medicine and so on. Nevertheless, a case can be made for introducing some of the day-to-day rigors to the potential practitioners, so their aspirations are based more on fact than romance. And, yes, I am speaking from my own personal experiences.

I encourage aspiring managers to focus as soon as possible on discovering some of the personal qualities essential for achieving executive-management success. Then, there needs to be a process of analyzing your own likes and dislikes—what makes you comfortable or uncomfortable—and thinking about whether this is a direction in which you really want to go. I know many attorneys who wish they hadn't become attorneys, dentists who wish they hadn't become dentists, etc. After getting into their professions, they discovered there were elements of the practice that made demands on them personally that created high levels of discomfiture and unhappiness. All of this is to say that a thorough evaluation of the personal demands involved in being a manager or executive ought to be taken into account before the decision becomes a serious mistake. The mentoring process is a very good process through which to explore this issue.

To do this, each aspirant should take a serious look at his own personality makeup in relation to career ambitions and then attempt to get some verification and affirmation about whether he's considering the right path. Probably the area that creates the most discomfort for managers and, consequently, one that they tend to avoid, is dealing with some of the human resource issues. These include areas such as improvement counseling, firing, conflict resolution and the like. Managing other people, with the demands inherent in dealing with various personalities and idiosyncrasies, is stressful and for some, beyond the responsibilities they could or would care to deal with. If this area of endeavor is something you just cannot come to grips with, then you should consider other options instead. An effective mentor can be of a lot of value in exploring this area.

WHAT MAKES A MANAGER?

It is always a great disappointment for me to find wonderful people who bear the title of manager when they don't know the first thing about it. How does it happen? Why do people get promoted to management positions who are so unprepared for the job of a manager?

It's because there is chaos at work in the business environment. You all know bad decisions get made and, in rapidly growing businesses, unfortunate shortcuts are taken by well-intentioned people in the process of promoting people into management slots. Sometimes I feel it would be a real benefit to receive a smack upside the head to remind us, one more time, before going through the management selection process and making an unprepared person into a manager, to ask whether he is really prepared to be one.

Maybe it also would be helpful, one more time, to look at what a manager does. I think we can all rely on Peter Drucker to give us a pretty good summary.

There are five basic responsibilities inherent in what a manager does:

1. *Sets objectives*—He determines what the goals and objectives should be in each area under his responsibility. He decides what has to be done to achieve these objectives. He makes the objectives effective by communicating them to the people whose cooperation and performance are required to attain them.

2. *Organizes*—He analyzes the activities, decisions and the various relations required to achieve the objectives. He then classifies the work, divides it into manageable activities and then into manageable jobs. He then selects the people for the responsibility to carry out these jobs.

3. *Motivates and communicates*—Now it's getting tougher. He then makes a team out of the people who are

responsible for the various jobs. He does that through the various practices he employs in order to manage. Essentially, it is done through a relationship with the people he manages. At the heart of this relationship process is the quality of the communication that supports the day-to-day relationship.

4 *The job of measurement*—Now it's getting even tougher yet. The manager has to establish some process. There are few factors that as are important to the performance of work than is the measurement of it. The effective manager will see that each person in the organization has measurements available to him that are focused on the performance of the whole organization and how that individual contributes to it. He will analyze performance, appraise it, interpret it and communicate the implications of the measurement to his colleagues.

5. *Develops people*—Through the way he manages, facilitating people to develop is either made easy or difficult. You can either direct people or misdirect them. He will either strengthen their integrity or corrupt it. He will either inspire them to become strong or he will contribute to their weaknesses.

Peter Drucker presented this information to the business world in 1955. And he is still right. Every manager does these things when he manages—whether he knows it or not. He may do them well or he may do them abysmally. But he always does them.

A manager is still a manager even though he carries out these functions poorly. But you can change that. And change it you must. Certainly, a person committed to becoming a mentor will be looking for areas to develop. I think you can safely start with Mr. Drucker's five basic elements of management and evaluate your prowess in these areas. Certainly, to further your career, performing these functions to the best of your abilities, and truly becoming practiced at it, will put you on the right path.

WHAT MAKES A MANAGER SUCCESSFUL?

Within the first year of my university graduation, one of my first managers introduced me to a concept that still rings true. This very wise gentleman, Joe Levitt, called me into his office one day and said, "Laddie, success is pleasing your boss." I thought about that for a moment and then realized he was saying that he was depending on my work to make him successful. And my work needed to be tuned-in to helping him achieve his goals. That was 1962. In 1992 Peter Drucker's *Managing for the Future.* was published. Thirty years later I was somewhat taken aback to see a very positive confirmation of what my old colleague, Joe, taught me. Mr. Drucker points out that there are few people as important to the performance and success of a manager as his boss. Drucker presents several ideas on how to manage the boss. But here's the nugget:

> The first 'Do' is to realize that it is both the subordinate's duty and in the subordinate's self-interest to make the boss as effective and as successful as possible. The best prescription for one's own success is still, after all, to work for a boss who is going places. Thus, the first 'Do' is to go to the boss—at least once a year—and ask, 'What do I do and what do my people do that helps *you* do your job? And what do I do that hampers *you* and makes life more difficult for *you*?'

Hey, Joe really got it right, didn't he? Well, this makes a lot of sense, but I'm afraid it's not put into practice often enough. All too often, you overlook the need and the opportunity to check in with the boss (even though this is a term a lot of us don't like, it still defines a very important role). It is an important step in your success to see what it is you are doing that is really helping "the boss" achieve his objectives. Managing the boss is a concept that has some unusual feelings attached to it. Rather than being a "boss," I prefer to view myself as a colleague who has a different job description that requires me to take responsibility for the actions of colleagues who report to me. Although they have a reporting responsibility, I avoid terms like "boss" and "subordinate" and prefer to describe their relationships in a more team/collegially oriented approach. Nevertheless, the concept is extremely valid.

Early in my career, I recall going to the manager I reported to and asking two questions. First, I wanted to know how I was doing. I wanted feedback. I wanted to know if I was doing the right things. And, second, I wanted to know what I could do to be better. I didn't realize it at the time but I was developing an approach that was going to carry my career forward in a fairly progressive way. I had discovered that my success really did depend on doing the right things, doing them well, and making sure I was supporting my colleague to whom I had a reporting responsibility. So, we come back to the question, what makes a manager successful?

Those five managerial functions need to be carried out very effectively. But then *effectively* needs to be defined by whether the effectiveness level is meeting the needs of senior management. Is it meeting the needs of your direct-report boss, who is responsible for your performance? One strategy that has served me well in helping those to whom I have reported has been a weekly one-on-one meeting initiated by me. I found that if I could have thirty minutes a week and prepare the agenda and cover that in an uninterrupted meeting with my superior that I could accomplish a number of things. They include:

◇ Maintaining awareness and keeping him informed of my overall activities. This supports the ethic of no surprises.

⋄ Look for feedback. This either will be confirmation or redirection to make sure that I'm on course.

⋄ Find out if there is anything I can do differently or better to meet the needs of the person I am trying to help be successful.

Then I turn this around in terms of meeting with the people who report to me. I coach and instruct them, communicating that, as their manager, my job is to help make them successful. If they are successful, then I get to be successful.

---- ◇ ----

The effective manager focuses on how he can make those above him, as well as those below him, as successful as possible.

---- ◇ ----

This introduces the phenomenon of *stewardship*. This is defined as the willingness to be accountable for results by operating in a *service* mode, rather than in a *control* mode, regarding those around us. Simply stated, it is accountability without control or compliance. This means that I am responsible for the best results I can help create.

PERSONAL ASSESSMENT

In order to create a clear direction for development of particular attributes, an evaluation of one's current performance should be done. A good process for commencing the evaluation process is the so-called "SWOT Analysis"—the acronym referred to earlier, which stands for Strengths, Weaknesses, Opportunities and Threats. A personal SWOT review, effectively administered, can make you aware of issues that deserve further evaluation. I listed some of the necessary characteristics for a leader-manager in Chapter Six. A conscientious evaluation of each of these areas could help identify strengths and weaknesses as well as talents and potential. There are a number of good psychometric measurement devices that can identify prowess or lack of it in these various performance areas. Also, this is an area in which it can be beneficial to use the resources of a professional human resources department. If I were setting out to establish a mentor/ mentee relationship and had just read the above material, I would be compelled to go to the HR director and ask him to help facilitate a process for an assessment of my strengths and weaknesses in these critical areas. Getting clarity on what specifically needs to be developed for future successes is at the core of a successful mentoring program. And I believe this is best implemented and managed by the mentee. Again, this comes back to the personal responsibility issue.

Looking back over my own career, I recall several incidents that triggered self-directed learning experiences. One that particularly stands out and which occurred very early in my career, was a public presentation I made where I felt I had done less than an outstanding job. Upon returning to my office and discussing the presentation with my colleagues, I received some support for my assessment. Therefore, I felt compelled to do something about it. Why? Deep down, I knew that if I were going to take my career as far as I could, this would be an area where I would have to improve. So, I did what I thought would create the best results.

As I shared earlier in this material, I signed on to teach a course in supervision at a local community college. After teaching for a couple of years, I learned to stand before a group of people and communicate comfortably. I'm sure that many of us have experienced business situations where the results were disappointing, and which triggered a desire to do something about it. If I had been mentored or evaluated by a colleague earlier, I might have come to the same conclusion. Instead, one of life's experiences brought it to my attention. A less embarrassing way to realize one's weaknesses is through a proactive mentoring process that facilitates planned growth and development, rather than waiting for crisis to provide the catalyst to react. A personal assessment that identifies talents, potential, unique aptitudes and the like can be a valuable process for planning one's development activities.

Early on in the mentoring process, the mentee inevitably comes to grips with the issue of his comfort zone. Various exercises and activities inevitably bring the mentee face-to-face with uncomfortable feelings about who he is and where he needs to go. The familiar expression so apt in sports, "no pain, no gain," also is valid for the field of management-development. True learning produces opportunities to use new skills before you feel completely confident. As a result, lag time between motivation and performance often occurs. Yet, through practice, skills and performance improve. None of us just got on a bicycle and took off down the road. The same is true in the development of one's management skills. It is necessary to move out of your comfort zone to achieve growth. Certainly, in my teaching role, my first few months of standing up in front of a class and delivering meaningful content was not easy. But as part of my development, it became easier with practice. And so it is with many things that managers do. But one has to discover what the elements for success are and then take steps to become a competent practitioner.

I've had the opportunity to observe a number of different types of corporate cultures. Some were most supportive of spawning self-guided personal development, while others were quite the contrary. For example, a manager or potential mentee who finds himself in a "command and control" environment tends to adapt to an autocratic style of governance and, as a result, spends his time watching and checking up on people so he can get as much as he can out of them. This tends to unintentionally produce an organization where people are passive, submissive and dependent. This is the type of environment one often finds in the strong entrepreneurially managed company, which includes a lot of the mid-market-sized businesses. Truly motivated managers, who wish to develop both personally and in their careers, find this kind of environment stifling. I've seen a lot of the brighter, more capable people move out of this type of culture in order to be able to grow their abilities and career.

The people I have seen who have been interested in developing their abilities tend to have a passion for knowledge and responsibility. It is an exciting thing to see and it usually happens in the more enlightened type of management culture.

THE OBJECTIVE

After the personal assessment has been completed, it's time for the mentee to take stock of where he's headed with his career. In the process, the kind of performance that will be expected of him, as well as the skills and abilities necessary for successful performance, will become clear.

If the mentee's targeted career coincides with opportunities where he currently works, then he can observe the performances of those who have the jobs. Hopefully, they are good role models.

Mentoring, however, usually takes on a much broader direction in terms of enhancing one's abilities to perform in a number of settings within the overall management framework. As noted earlier, mentoring by definition tends to be a broader developmental track than coaching, which provides specific skills enhancement. The main issue is to identify the areas where the mentee should focus in order to develop his career. This process should be undertaken annually, at least. As the mentee hones his performance abilities, and his knowledge and understanding of management, other areas of interest and concern will emerge.

What the mentee should bring to the mentor is a general description or desire regarding what he hopes to accomplish by being mentored. This, then, can help the mentor prepare material for discussion, for reading, and for general developmental purposes that will be tailored to the mentee's needs. Having said that, if the mentoring program is one that is established and sponsored by the company, then there may well be certain materials and content that the sponsors will have included for the mentees. If that's the case, I would trust that the mentee would be able to assess the material and determine where to apply the greatest focus for his benefit.

The key point here is that the mentee needs to be prepared to offer some direction in pursuit of his own development. He should have a general impression of areas to strengthen or competencies to gain. Moreover, as he contemplates career growth, he should have certain management aspirations in mind for which he is preparing himself. This provides excellent discussion material between the mentor and mentee for overall development planning. Taking charge of one's career direction and executing a development strategy can be greatly enhanced through the mentoring process.

MENTOR'S CHECKUP

◇ What are you doing to keep up with the rapid changes occurring in the business place?

◇ Have you thought about what knowledge or skills will be required to be highly effective in your job next year? Five years from now?

◇ Would it be wise for you to initiate a dialogue with your reporting superior to determine what else you could be doing to help him or her be more effective?

◇ Is your career going in the direction you want? What else can you do?

CHAPTER FOURTEEN

MENTORING EFFECTIVE TRANSITION

OVERVIEW

Recently, a project that I had been working on resulted in a meeting with a number of bankers and former bankers. Naturally, the conversation got around to the amount of change their industry has been experiencing. Massive. That is the only word that does justice to the banking revolution of the past couple of years. And it's not over. Similar changes are occurring in other industries, too. I'm sure that being over fifty adds to my perception of the rate at which change is occurring. Regardless, it's now an issue every business leader must confront sooner or later.

Even some of the very large businesses, such as GE, are adopting "small company" strategies that are based on flexibility. Flexibility and quickness are requirements for remaining competitive. Having a "flex/quick" capability means the business has to be lean, agile and smart. And no dozing will be tolerated.

Creating a preferred business future will be the result of a well-executed strategy. Accomplishing such a feat most likely will be accompanied by a change in the business culture. There are three essential focus points that facilitate significant cultural change: empowerment, community and collaboration. The product of this process is a proliferation of workleaders, the people responsible for producing exceptional results. And how can this all get accomplished? Through mentoring.

THE FUTURE OF MANAGEMENT LEADERSHIP

As you arrive at the last chapter of this book, it seems worthwhile to consider what is happening in the global marketplace and what the emerging successful strategies are. What I see firmly convinces me that the mentoring strategy developed thus far is absolutely on track. Comprehensive mentoring aimed at learning, leading and relating can help a company create the kind of top-performance culture needed to rapidly respond to changing environments.

THE GLOBAL MARKETPLACE

Successful managers must stay on top of what is occurring in the global marketplace. Virtually all U.S. businesses are impacted by the new global economy. During my recent residence in the U.K., the same conclusion was inescapable. The international economic variables that can and do impact a business seem to be increasing exponentially, and keeping tabs on the competition has become incredibly complex—you are never sure who the competition may be next week.

What has become clear is that every organization must be stripped down for action, relieved of excess baggage and made capable of moving quickly. To become flexible and quick has required major rethinking about traditional management models. This is particularly true for larger businesses. It is tough enough to get even some mid-market businesses I have encountered to respond in "cut time." Bigger businesses make it more complex. However, there are some outstanding examples of big companies responding with the new "flex/quick" corporate strategy. Being large does not have to equate with "rigid/slow." If this becomes the case, the marketplace will deal with it, if it hasn't already.

FLEX/QUICK-MANAGEMENT/LEADERSHIP

An excellent current example of a big company functioning like a smaller company is General Electric. John Welch, Jr. is chairman and CEO of GE. His successful leadership strategy is based on what he calls "body of big, soul of small." In the company's 1995 Annual Report, he described the new kind of company the GE executive team had begun and would continue to develop. These were the salient features of that new strategy:

a. *Changing the hardware*–There were two critical moves. First was the elimination of business units that were not contributing at a "market leader" level. Second was the pruning of what Welch called the "corporate underbrush." These were the traditional corporate bureaucratic units that provided big company evaluation and direction, yet frequently slowed the decision-making process significantly. With this change, operating units were empowered and charged to be more independent.

b. *Changing the software*–This change was aimed at creating the small company culture. Three cultural elements were targeted: self-confidence, simplicity and speed. Self-confidence was cultivated by encouraging leadership throughout the organization. Simplicity was encouraged by asking leaders to produce simple plans, speak simply and propose big, clear targets. Speed was encouraged based on the success of the simplification processes and a shared sense of urgency.

c. *Involving everyone*–This was a basic empowerment move to achieve the "my company" feeling. And this is most effectively achieved through true, real involvement. This type of involvement was accomplished through what was termed "Work-Out" meetings. Based on getting the people closest to the work involved in its direction, Work-Out sessions became the source of creative management.

d. *Promoting boundary-less behavior*–Welch reports the sweetest fruit of boundary-less behavior has been the demise of "not-invented-here" type thinking. Learning from each other, looking for ideas and emphasizing integrated diversity has worked. Another significant contributor has been the stock-option compensation program, which really underscored the "we" element of the culture.

Welch concluded his annual report that year with the observation that they had created a new kind of company at GE. The new company embodies all the strengths of the big company while moving with the hunger, speed and urgency of a small company.

It took more than five years to change the culture at GE to achieve the quick and flexible culture. For a company that size, that is incredibly fast and is a real tribute to the leadership. And that is exactly what was required—committed, visionary leadership. More and more, this is the kind of leadership that is required to effectively compete in the global marketplace.

Dynamic Transition

A New Culture

What Welch has done at GE essentially is happening in some form in most successful, high-tech companies today. The environment demands it. Traditional management models just don't work. A new corporate culture, or a reinvented one, that is focused on facilitating dynamic transition is the new, effective model. The current focus is on the rapid change in high technology companies. While the change rate generally is greater for the high-tech companies, all businesses face it at some level.

───── ◇ ─────

It will be difficult, if not impossible, for any company to escape the impact of the global marketplace.

───── ◇ ─────

Thus, a new management model is worthy of consideration, if not crucial for survival, for all businesses. Orchestrating a culture and management-style change of the magnitude discussed so far requires a comprehensive approach. Following are three essential action points to facilitate culture change aimed at producing exceptional results.

a. *Empowerment*—The new business model for dynamic transition has as its central focus empowerment. Unfortunately, the word "empowerment" has been so popularized in management writing over the past several years that it now carries some emotional baggage. If someone mentions empowerment, I fear that many feel, "Oh, not that again" or "We've been there, done that." Like so many popular concepts that are rarely thoroughly and effectively implemented, empowerment cannot be partially implemented. It's like being slightly pregnant. Implementing an empowerment process requires absolute resolve. I'm certain John Welch or anyone on his management team could verify this. Experiences in the organizations I have managed absolutely support this conclusion.

I have introduced the empowerment concept to the management cultures of several mid-sized companies and I'm here to tell you that it takes time, forethought, planning, preparation and skilled implementation. Empowerment is the means to the end, not the end itself. It is the means through which leadership is distributed. The empowerment process can facilitate the distribution of leadership skills but it will not create the skills themselves. I'm sure that was true at GE and other organizations that utilize empowerment to disburse leadership.

b. *Community*–Another concept of strengthened relationships that produce new synergy for better results is described as "community." Traditional organizational concepts and practices have created barriers to cooperation and communication. Under a community approach, an emphasis is placed on interdependence rather than independence. While empowerment strengthens leadership, community strengthens communication and understanding, two essential elements of culture building.

c. *Collaboration*–The importance of cooperation rather than competition is stressed in a collaborative process. Competition is fierce enough in the marketplace without having to confront it in the developmental processes of business. Encouraging participative problem resolution and tapping into heretofore unused resources has produced some amazing accomplishments. In particular, I suggest reading Masaaki Imai's description of the benefits of collaboration in his landmark book, *Kaizen: The Key to Japan's Competitive Success.*

MENTORING THE MODEL

To draw upon the benefits of empowerment, community and collaboration, proficient leadership and relationship skills must already be in place and readily accessible. Empowerment facilitates leaders and leaders create the future. And what is the description of your most effective leader-prototype? One who is involved in continuous learning, developing leadership and social skills. This is how you develop a company of *workleaders.* And the most effective strategy for accomplishing this feat is the Strategic Mentoring Model.

To change a culture requires profound focus and commitment. The process has to "touch" all aspects of the organization. New thinking, new attitudes, new processes are all involved. Making massive attitudinal adjustments represents perhaps *the* most difficult under-taking for business leadership. Think about it. John Welch couldn't sit across the desk from 222,000 fellow employees and sell them on the new culture. It took a very big team several years; and the job is never done. As employees come and go, the new participants have to "go to class" to understand the cultural software that really does drive the business. And the most effective software implementation and maintenance system I have found is continuous mentoring.

The dilemma that I see is this: Cultural change takes concentrated effort. I firmly believe it takes the CEO to drive it. If the CEO is not committed and involved in a highly visible way, optimal results will not be realized. This is one program that cannot begin from the bottom and bubble up. The senior management leadership must become an integral part of the culture's redevelopment and the accompanying transition phase necessary to redefine the business and its processes. A proactive transition and development strategy prepares a business to address marketplace demands and opportunities. And leadership from the top is essential.

TRANSITION AND DEVELOPMENTAL MANAGEMENT

OPPORTUNITY SPOTTING

New opportunities will be found by those prepared to find them. And that, dear colleagues, is the future of business. New opportunities are the lifeblood of businesses involved in competitive markets. A good friend and colleague in the U.K., Nigel MacLennan, wrote a fascinating book that was recently published on this subject titled *Opportunity Spotting.* Nigel has some wonderful suggestions on how businesses can develop their creative processes to be better opportunity spotters. He also provides some creative exercises to develop more sensitive "antennae" to help spot opportunities. Essentially, spotting them boils down to being prepared. It really needs to be a part of the continuous learning processes of the business. And that's the most effective kind of transition management, one based on developing its human resources to lead the transition rather than simply reacting to it.

WORKLEADERS UNDER DEVELOPMENT

By now you can see where you are heading. Can you just imagine an organization chocked-full of empowered workleaders? A management hierarchy is still needed, but much of the hierarchy's purpose will be realized through senior management facilitation and coordination of workleader contributions. Add to that the oversight of the workleader mentoring program, which equates to the Strategic Mentoring Model.

One of senior management's major responsibilities is to work "on" the business as opposed to working "in" the business. This focus supports the development of workleaders. Multiplying the number of participants involved in looking for opportunities to do business better and to find new sources of business is what will create future business success. Let's look at how this impacts the core competencies of the business.

MEETING FUTURE MARKETPLACE DEMANDS

Gary Hamel and C.K. Prahalad's book, *Competing for the Future,* convincingly highlights the need for businesses to understand their core competencies. Once understood, these competencies need to be nurtured and developed to strategically manage the "knowledge resources" of businesses to successfully compete in and for the future. Hamel and Prahalad identify five key competence management tasks: (1) identifying existing core competencies; (2) establishing a core competence acquisition agenda; (3) building core competencies; (4) deploying core competencies; and (5) protecting and defending core competence leadership.

Frankly, I think the most effective way of achieving core competence leadership is by mentoring workleaders through the Strategic Mentoring Model. Focusing on mentoring learning, leading and relating toward building leadership in core competencies is what creates the preferred future.

MENTORING FROM THE TOP

Executives in an organization are in the best position to understand what is needed by their colleagues in order to expand their abilities. The chief executive and the senior management team are responsible for the growth and development of management within the enterprise. After all, it is the management structure that executives must work through to achieve the corporate objectives. Should they not then be focusing on building this resource to optimize its performance? Of course. However, all too often I've seen the pressures of the day robbing senior management of the vision and drive to create this kind of focus. It is very much the responsibility of senior management to be working "on" the business more than they are working "in" the business. Working on enhancing the skills, abilities and growth of management personnel is one of the highest payoff areas there is. So, how should you proceed?

As discussed in Chapter Eight, the chief executive is the prime sponsor of the corporate culture. It's his actions, programs and strategies that create much of the corporate personality. If he emphasizes the importance of a learning organization and encourages his senior management colleagues to be personally involved in growth activities, then you are going to see an organization in growth. What a fantastic resource it represents for a chief executive to sponsor a mentoring culture that enforces and reinforces the wisdom of a growth strategy.

I first started mentoring small groups by suggesting that new managers read Drucker's *Managing for Results,* followed by an invitation to have dinner together to discuss it. Within a few years this caught on and several cells within the company were emulating that example, as well as the occasional one-on-one mentoring sessions.

Through such activities, the chief executive alerts everybody to the fact that learning and growing are important.

The chief executive has the tremendous opportunity to see that mentoring becomes part of the corporate culture. The strategy that seems to make the most sense is to create a network of mentors who generally follow a development strategy created by senior management and human resources. In this regard, it may be wise to engage the services of a development specialist, an outside consultant, to assist in the design and launch of such a system. This presents an excellent opportunity for the enterprise to conduct an executive assessment. Based on the results of the carefully executed assessment, a strategy can be developed for each participant to enhance further growth and development.

SKILLS ASSESSMENT

Larger organizations with well-staffed human resource departments may well have the resident skills to perform an executive assessment. Essentially, this is a process designed to administer a type of measurement process that ascertains strengths and weaknesses of the senior management group in terms of their overall management skills. While this sounds potentially threatening, it can be carried off in a way that can produce some rather exciting results. Ultimately, the goal is to increase effectiveness. You do this in management development by strengthening those areas where performance could be enhanced. Yes, it is a sensitive area, but there are sensitive ways to deal with it. That's why it can often be better executed by an outside expert than by the resident human resource staff.

Engaging specialists to assist in the development and implementation of a comprehensive mentoring plan can create very significant benefits. Focusing on the right training and developmental elements, rather than a shotgun approach, will produce many more valuable results for the short term.

The concept of using an outsider to launch such a program has real merit. There is so much at stake it would be unfortunate to not develop the most effective program from the outset. The chances of this happening with inside staff, while not out of the question, may not be as forthcoming. There are specialists who perform these types of services, who are knowledgeable and practiced at implementing and assisting in the maintenance of these types of programs. Getting their involvement in the design and then later assessing the results can keep the program on course in accomplishing better results. There is such a huge opportunity to achieve so many beneficial results that the planning and implementation must reflect that magnitude of opportunity.

Continuing the theme that the emphasis should come from the top, the consultant should work essentially with the CEO and the HR executive in developing such a program. If the program is viewed in any way as not having the full support and weight of the chief executive, then the results will suffer accordingly.

THE CONSULTANT'S ROLE

In order to launch an effective mentoring strategy, one approach that makes a lot of sense is to begin with an assessment of the senior management team. What do they need to be concentrating on to increase their effectiveness? There are some fairly impressive management tools that can be used to measure the overall effectiveness of the team and each of its members. Comprehensive assessments that I'm familiar with have provided some very useful information for preparing an overall executive development strategy.

Each of us has responsibility for our own growth. Yet having said that, I want to do everything I can as a chief executive to make sure that I facilitate that process. Sure, we all know what we ought to do; it's the follow-through that really separates the high-achievers from the rest of the pack. There aren't that many high-achievers and there sure aren't enough to go around. So, I would like to help as many of my achievers as possible to become high-achievers. What has worked for me is to support their efforts in their growth processes. If I can be a facilitator and an encourager then we all win.

CONSULTANT AS MENTOR

Another role I've seen played by a consultant is a mentoring role to the chief executive. Early in this book, I noted that I satisfied this need in my own career with an outside mentor. The problem that the CEO often has is that he really has no one within the organization who can meet his needs as a mentor. He has to "go to the well" someplace; often this can be fulfilled with a mentor-consultant. As a CEO, I am responsible not only for my own growth but for encouraging the growth in others. As a part of my own personal growth, I have tried to address my needs, as much as possible, through dealing with issues at hand. This often results in the need to discuss issues with a party that can function as a sounding board. Finding someone who has the experience base to provide new insights into the issues of the moment, stimulate new thinking and even provide suggestions for added information can be of great value.

For those of us who function in the role of CEO, you know there are times when your sources of inspiration in dealing with pressing issues feel limited. I'm not talking about a counselor who puts me on the couch. I'm talking about a counselor/mentor who has perspective on me and my organization and who can help trigger productive thinking when I may be stuck on a particular issue. I have experienced the situation and I have experienced the benefit of a mentor, and I know that it's a tremendous resource. Having a mentor work with me in my organizational context has proven to be a valuable process for both myself and the organization. Of course, the success of the endeavor required my having chosen a mentor who was capable of addressing the magnitude of the issues that I needed to have addressed. The buck stopped with me on that one.

The management-development function of the company is a fertile investment area. Getting it right has numerous benefits, obviously. Finding a mentor who can truly add value is a tremendous asset. Because of the responsibilities and the types of issues, I would want my mentor to actually have had management experience himself in an operating environment. I do not want to take away from your learned colleagues who are in the teaching profession, for they add much to your overall management knowledge. For my own needs, however, I have found a greater value in working with someone who has had similar responsibilities. For example, those who have had similar experiences, such as bottom-line responsibilities, have a common dimension in their understanding. This can contribute much to rapport and empathy. I want to work with a mentor who has awakened in the middle of the night in a cold sweat over some particular management or operating problem, like I have; someone who's had to deal with pressing management issues. Practical experience in the trenches can add another quite valuable dimension to the mentoring perspective.

WISDOM AND MENTORING

At the outset of this book, I discussed the origins of mentoring. In particular, I referred to the wisdom literature found in the Old Testament, specifically the book of Proverbs. A particular verse in Proverbs has a timeless message in support of mentoring:

A wise man will hear and increase in learning,
and a man of understanding will acquire wise counsel.

–Proverbs 1:5

As I contemplated historical wisdom literature and early evidence of mentoring, I developed a keen appreciation for the role of wisdom in mentoring. In fact, without wisdom, mentoring is folly. The following acronym took shape in looking at the application of wisdom in the process of mentoring.

WINNING

INVESTING

SPECIAL

DYNAMIC

ORGANIZATION

MENTOR

Winning–Everybody loves to win. Winning is far more fun, exciting and rewarding than losing. But it usually takes extra effort and preparation. Sometimes it is not clear what to do. And when it is, you come to the effort part. That often escapes people as well. A close look at winners usually reveals that they have successfully dealt with both parts of this equation—knowing what to do and then doing it. It's the old combination of knowledge and performance. When winners achieve Olympic standing, then you can be fairly certain that coaching and mentoring had a role in the process. Mentoring produces winners. A winning business only becomes so through the performance of its winners.

Investing—What you invest your time and talents in is where you see a return. Mentoring is investing. Investing in the development of your human resources offers a potential return on investment of the highest magnitude. Your people are your greatest asset and, if it is possible, are becoming even more so. The future depends on the quality of your human resources. How can you *not* make the investment?

Special—There is a part of every one of us that likes special treatment. That's the major ingredient in the whole customer service revolution of the past two decades. You want to be special—or at least be treated that way. In the mentoring process you focus "special" attention on your colleagues through assisting them in their growth and development. You want them to be special. And that realization for those being mentored has a tremendous positive impact on the achievement of special results.

Dynamic—Change is happening so fast that I fear what I learned yesterday may be terribly dated next week. An exaggeration? Not in some environments. Fortunately, not all business environments are quite that dynamic. However, it's just a matter of degree. You have to approach most business environments on the basis that something new is happening or can happen every day. Adding understanding to change requires continuous learning. Meeting the heightened demands resulting from change requires more leadership. Working together to address these growing challenges requires better relationship skills. The needs of the people involved in this dynamic culture are oriented around growth. This type of growth is best nurtured and developed through mentoring.

Organization—New problems/opportunities require new methods. Many businesses keep using the same strategies they have used for years, yet keep hoping to produce different results. A new organizational model is emerging—one that is change-friendly. It's sleeker, smarter and more agile. Or it's in the process of becoming so in order to survive the decade. But you want more than survival—you want exceptional performance. Mentoring can enable just that.

Mentor—In case you hadn't noticed, that's "me" in the word "mentor." The "me" requires a lot of wisdom to balance the various forces needed to make a mentoring program effective. First, as a CEO, I need to be involved in mentoring—the first "me" in mentoring. But there can't be too much of me or the effectiveness will be greatly reduced. Mentors facilitate, not dictate. Guidance is the key. Too much guidance becomes direction and the growth aspects of the process can be severely diminished when this happens. The second application of "me" in mentoring can and should take a stronger role than simply guidance. And that has to do with facilitating the mentoring program organization-wide, actually creating culture. This must bear the identity of the CEO.

I am firmly convinced that to effectively manage change now requires the mentoring of growth. To mentor an organization effectively requires the application of many disciplines: Chief among them is wisdom. The quest for wisdom usually has led me to a mentor.

MENTOR'S CHECKUP

◇ How agile is your organization in responding to change? What mechanisms do you have in place as your "early warning system" regarding marketplace demands?

◇ How is the culture of your organization evolving? Is there a strategy in place?

◇ How well does the concept of workleaders—every worker leading and every leader working—apply to your environment?

◇ What is the worst thing that could happen to your business? Have you developed contingency plans?

REFERENCES

Adair, John. *Developing Leaders: The Ten Key Principles.* New York: McGraw-Hill, 1989.

Adizes, Ichak. *Mastering Change: The Power of Mutual Trust and Respect in Personal Life, Business and Society.* Santa Monica, CA: Adizes Institute Publications, 1991.

Belasco, James. *Teaching the Elephant to Dance—Empowering Change in Your Organization.* New York: Crown, 1990.

Belasco, James and Ralph Stayer. *Flight of the Buffalo.* New York: Warner Brooks, 1994.

Belbin, R. Meredith. *Management Teams.* Oxford, UK: Butterworth-Heineman, 1981.

Bell, Chip. *Managers As Mentors: Building Partnerships for Learning.* San Francisco, CA: Berrett-Koehler, 1996.

Bennet, Robert F. *Gaining Control: Your Key to Freedom and Success.* Salt Lake City, UT: Franklin International Institute, 1987.

Bennis, Warren and Burt Nannus. *Leaders: Strategies for Taking Charge.* New York: Harper Collins, 1997.

Block, Peter. *Stewardship: Choosing Service over Self-Interest.* San Francisco, CA: Berrett-Koehler, 1993.

Cluterbuck, David. *Everyone Needs a Mentor.* London: I.P.D., 1991.

Collins, James and Jerry Porras. *Built to Last—Successful Habits of Visionary Companies.* New York: Harper Collins, 1994.

Covey, Stephen. *The 7 Habits of Highly Effective People: Powerful Lessons in Personal Change.* Hamden, CT: Fireside, 1990.

Daniels, Aubrey. *Bringing Out the Best in People: How to Apply the Astonishing Power of Positive Reinforcement.* New York: McGraw-Hill, 1993.

Dilts, Robert and Gino Bonissone. *Skills for the Future— Managing Creativity and Innovation.* Cupertino, CA: Meta Publications, 1993.

Drucker, Peter F. *Managing for Results: Economic Tasks and Risk-Taking Decisions.* New York: Harper Collins, 1993.

―――. *Managing for the Future: The 1990s and Beyond.* New York: Plume, an imprint of New American Library, 1993.

―――. *The Practice of Management.* New York: Harper Collins, 1993.

Eccles, Tony. *Succeeding with Change—Implementing Action-Driven Strategies.* Cambridge, MA: Harvard Business School Press, 1996.

Gates, Bill. *The Road Ahead.* New York: Viking, 1996.

Gerber, Michael. *The E-Myth Revisited: Why Most Small Businesses Don't Work and What to Do About It.* New York: Harper Collins, 1995.

General Electric Company. *Annual Report.* Fairfield, CT: General Electric Company, 1996.

Goldratt, Eliyahu, and Jeff Cox. *The Goal: A Process of Ongoing Improvement.* Croton-on-Hudson, NY: North River Press, 1994.

Goleman, Daniel. *Emotional Intelligence.* New York: Bantam Doubleday Dell, 1997.

Greenleaf, Robert. *Servant Leadership: A Journey into the Nature of Legitimate Power and Greatness.* New York: Paulist Press, 1983.

Hamel, Gary and C.K. Prahalad. *Competing for the Future.* New York: McGraw-Hill, 1994.

Hargrove, Robert. *Masterful Coaching: Extraordinary Results by Impacting People and the Way They Think and Work Together.* San Diego, CA: Pfeiffer & Co., 1995.

Harrison, Roger. *Leadership and Strategy for a New Age: Lessons from 'Conscious Evolution.'* Menlo Park, CA: SRI International, 1982.

Hay, Julie. *Transformational Mentoring: Creating Developmental Alliances for Changing Organizational Cultures.* London: McGraw-Hill, 1995.

Hill, Charles, and Gareth Jones, *Strategic Management: An Integrated Approach.* Boston, MA: Houghton Mifflin, 1991.

Hunsaker, Phillip, and Anthony Alessandra, The Art of Managing People. New York: Simon & Schuster, 1986.

Imai, Masaaki. *Kaizen: The Key to Japan's Competitive Success.* New York: McGraw-Hill, 1989.

Jung, Carl Gustav. *Psychological Types.* [vol. 6]. Princeton, NJ: Princeton University Press, 1971.

Kanter, Rosabeth Moss. *The Change Masters: Innovation and Entrepreneurship in the American Corporation.* New York: Simon & Schuster, 1985.

Kotter, John, and James Heskett. *Corporate Culture and Performance.* Riverside, NJ: Free Press, 1992.

Lessem, Ronnie. *Business as a Learning Community.* New York: McGraw-Hill, 1993.

MacLennan, Nigel. *Coaching and Mentoring*. Aldershot, Haunts, UK: Ashgate Publishing, 1995.

MacLennan, Nigel. *Opportunity Spotting*. Aldershot, Haunts, UK: Ashgate Publishing, 1994.

Mellander, Klas. *The Power of Learning: Fostering Employee Growth*. Homewood, IL: A.S.T.D., 1993.

Mintzberg, Henry, and James Quinn. *The Strategy Process—Concepts, Contexts and Cases*. 3rd. ed. Upper Saddle River, NJ: Prentice-Hall, 1996.

Murphy, Emmett. *Leadership IQ: A Personal Development Process Based on a Scientific Study of a New Generation of Leaders*. John Wiley & Sons, New York: 1996.

Musgrave, James, and Michael Anniss. *Relationship Dynamics: Theory and Analysis*. Riverside, NJ: Free Press, 1996.

Napuk, Kerry. *The Strategy-Led Business: Step-By-Step Planning for Your Company's Future*. New York: McGraw-Hill, 1993.

Oliver, Eric. *The Human Factor at Work: A Guide to Self-Reliance and Consumer Protection for the Mind*. Canton, MI: MetaSystems, 1993.

Parsloe, Eric. *Coaching, Mentoring and Assessing: A Practical Guide to Developing Competence*. London: Kogan Page, 1995.

Pascale, Richard. "Perspectives on Strategy: The Real Story Behind Honda's Success." *California Management Review* 26, 1984.

Pearson, Gordon. *The Competitive Organization: Managing for Organizational Excellence*. Henley Management Series. London: McGraw-Hill, 1992.

Pedler, Mike, John Burgoyne and Tom Boydell, *A Manager's Guide to Self-Development*. McGraw-Hill Self-Development [Series]. London: McGraw-Hill, 1994.

Robert, Michel. *Strategy, Pure and Simple: How Winning CEOs Outthink Their Competition*. McGraw-Hill, New York: 1993.

Senge, Peter. *The Fifth Discipline: The Art and Practice of the Learning Organization*. Doubleday, New York: 1994.

Thorne, Paul. *Organizing Genius—The Pursuit of Corporate Creativity and Innovation*. Cambridge, MA: Blackwell, 1993.

Thurow, Lester. *Head to Head: The Coming Economic Battle Among Japan, Europe, and America*. New York: Warner Books, 1993.

Tobin, Daniel. *Transformational Learning: Renewing Your Company Through Knowledge and Skills*. New York: John Wiley & Sons, 1996.

"Work Week," *Wall Street Journal*. Dec. 12, 1995, p.1.

ENDNOTE

Well, there you have it. In these mere three hundred-plus pages I have shared my passion for excellence through mentoring. It can make a significant difference to an individual, an executive team and an entire business. A difference that can place and keep you in the winner's circle. As you make decisions regarding how to proceed in your business and personal life with processes that produce high-impact success, my belief is that mentoring is what will make it possible. My wish for corporate America is that it embrace widespread strategic mentoring—at every level. The result? There will be only winners.

Here's to exceptional performance through mentoring.

Hal Johnson

Note: The author may be reached by e-mail at mentorwrks@aol.com or by fax at (800) 247-9555.

ABOUT THE AUTHOR

Upon graduating from the University of Southern California in 1961 with a Bachelor's Degree in Social Science, Hal Johnson began his career with the City of Los Angeles Budget Office. There he spent nine years developing his management abilities through increasingly responsible assignments. During this period, he received a full-tuition scholarship that enabled him to earn a Master of Public Administration Degree.

In 1971, he became the first director of management services for the city of Portland in the newly centralized finance and administration office. Four years later, he moved to the private sector and began focusing on transitioning companies into management cultures based on shared management and leadership principles, emphasizing high performance.

For the subsequent twenty-plus years, Hal served as CEO in five different companies, generally transitioning organizations from entrepreneurial to team-management cultures, with special emphasis on work measurement, personnel development and performance. Most recently, he served as CEO of Transax PLC, based in Birmingham, England, Europe's largest check guarantee company.

In the course of becoming a business-transition specialist, he has developed a unique and effective mentoring strategy that enables companies to develop their human resources to achieve exceptional performance.

In addition to serving on several boards of directors, Hal is Managing Director of Private Capital Northwest and President of MentoringWorks, Inc. He serves as a consultant, writer and lecturer, both domestically and internationally. He resides with his wife, Adeline, in the farm country outside Portland, Oregon. They met in high school and are celebrating their thirty-eighth wedding anniversary this year. They are the parents of a married son, Brad (wife—Joy), a married daughter, Michelle (husband—Kevin), and have two grandchildren, Rachel and Kyle.